BEFORE
YOU SAY
"I QUIT!"

BEFORE YOU SAY "I QUIT!"

A Guide to Making Successful
Job Transitions

Diane Holloway, Ph.D.
and
Nancy Bishop

COLLIER BOOKS

Macmillan Publishing Company

NEW YORK

To those who never quit supporting this book:
Kathe Telingator, Mitch Lobrovich, Bob Cheney,
Richard Citrin, Ph.D., and Margaret Pinder, Ph.D.

Copyright © 1990 by Diane Holloway and Nancy Bishop

Collier Books
Macmillan Publishing Company
866 Third Avenue, New York, NY 10022
Collier Macmillan Canada, Inc.

Library of Congress Cataloging-in-Publication Data
Holloway, Diane.
Before you say "I quit!" : a guide to making successful job
transitions / Diane Holloway and Nancy Bishop.
p. cm.
Includes bibliographical references.
ISBN 0-02-076881-8
1. Career changes. I. Bishop, Nancy, 1949– . II. Title.
HF5384.H65 1990
650.14—dc20 89-22388 CIP

Macmillan books are available at special discounts for bulk
purchases for sales promotions, premiums, fund-raising, or
educational use.
For details, contact:

Special Sales Director
Macmillan Publishing Company
866 Third Avenue
New York, NY 10022

Design by Ellen R. Sasahara

10 9 8 7 6 5 4 3 2

PRINTED IN THE UNITED STATES OF AMERICA

Contents

Contents

* A guide to drawing up a list of job options by using six basic considerations

Contents

Introduction

YOU'VE had it. Your boss is unreasonable, you dislike your work, and your career seems to be going nowhere. As you fantasize about resigning, you see yourself march into the boss's office, shut the door, and with all the chutzpah of Johnny Paycheck singing "Take This Job and Shove It," you announce, "I quit!"

Then what?

That's the question people often ask too late. At least 25 percent of all American workers are dissatisfied with their jobs,[1] and ten million people will actually resign this year.[2] Most will see leaving their jobs as an end to their problems.

Unfortunately, a large number of these people will continue in a frustrating cycle of unsatisfying jobs. And it won't be because they lack the skills, intelligence, or the will to find something better. They will fail to do better because they'll simply bail out, without understanding what went wrong, what would make them happier, and how to get it. Acting without sufficient self-knowledge or a game plan, they'll find that events are controlling them instead of the other way around.

If you've picked up this book, chances are you're wrestling with job problems and may be on the verge of quitting. Perhaps you're wondering whether telling your boss to "shove it" is the best thing to do.

You may feel like Robert, a man I counseled, who didn't know what move to make next. Robert was a young newspaper reporter at a major metropolitan daily. After eighteen months of tolerating editors whom he thought were abusive and marginally competent, he decided he'd had enough and turned in his two weeks' notice. His immediate feeling was one of vindication and relief. He wasn't concerned about finding another job, even though he had nothing definite lined up. He had a few promising leads and a little money in the bank.

It took him three months to find a position on another newspaper, despite the fact that he had an impressive résumé. By the time he was offered a job, he was ready to take anything, and he did—a position at a publication with less prestige and lower circulation and at a little less pay than the position he'd quit.

After a while, Robert noticed he was having the same problems with his new editors. That's when he sought counseling. He said he was frustrated, angry, and ready to tell off the city editor, but he realized he might face another long stretch of unemployment. He wanted help in dealing with the situation because he believed a career in journalism was right for him.

Robert and I then began a process that has proved successful time and again in helping people resolve unhappy work situations. First, I helped him refocus his thinking, so he was approaching the problem from a position of control rather than helplessness. Believe me, the situation is never as hopeless as you may think it is. Then we examined all the problems—the sources of pain and the possible reasons these situations were arising. We looked below the surface at possible underlying reasons for his unhappiness.

After going through many of the basic steps that are described in this book, Robert realized that he was more interested in writing than he was in reporting. And while he had some legitimate complaints against his editors, they were justified in criticizing his slowness—he had difficulty cranking out a story fast enough for the requirements of daily deadlines. He was a perfectionist who would spend a long time polishing each article. Even though he had been working at it, he realized he simply wasn't going to produce any faster.

For the first time, he understood clearly where he belonged. "What I really need to do," he said, smiling at what now seemed obvious to him, "is work on a magazine. I've toyed with the idea, but now I see that's *it*. I'd have more time to write the type of stories I really enjoy."

With a better understanding of himself and a clearly defined goal, Robert was able to go back to work with renewed vigor. He proposed story ideas to the city editor that would allow him to do longer, magazine-style pieces and showcase his writing skills. He targeted a magazine where he wanted to work. Being realistic—not starting with *Esquire*, which was at the top of his list—he chose a city magazine with a very good reputation. Finally, based on the strength of articles he'd written and on his ideas for other stories, he got a job there.

Making a career shift within his field was Robert's solution. For someone else, it might have been switching to a copy-editing position, going into the broadcast side of the business, getting into a new field altogether, or simply staying put—which brings us to the essence of this book.

Before You Say "I Quit!" isn't simply a tool to help you quit. It's designed to help you make the right choice—including the possibility of staying right where you are—at a critical juncture in your work life. In a survey we made of employers selected for *The 100 Best Companies to Work for in America,* 73 percent reported that the most common mistake unhappy employees make is to not try to work out problems before they quit.

An exasperated personnel director for a major food distributor was speaking for many of his colleagues when he said, "Employees often quit before giving us a chance to see if we can do something to improve their situation. We might have been able to make changes if they had discussed the matter with us."

Often people base their decision to quit on emotions rather than logic. Kurtis Kishi, professional staffing and employment manager of Walt Disney Studios in Burbank, California, told us, "If you look back on the early stages of your career, you can probably find one or two examples of acting more emotionally than logically. You may decide they're not paying you enough and get angry and feel like you've been mistreated."

Before You Say "I Quit!" provides an organized approach to deciding if quitting is the best choice for you and the steps to take to implement your decision. Because the average person may have ten or more jobs during a lifetime,[3] knowing how to go about quitting a job—to make an effective transition—is as critical as knowing how to find employment.

By following the step-by-step process in this book, you'll learn how to:

- Regain control of your work life
- Determine the real source of your job dissatisfaction (which often is not as obvious as it may seem)
- Develop more job options than you initially thought were available to you
- Consider whether a career change is your best alternative
- Consider your options and job offers through a systematic evaluation process
- Decide whether to quit or keep your job
- Stay and improve your job if it's in your best interest

- Resign in such a way that you make a smooth transition to your next job if that's preferable
- Handle a job interviewer's questions about why you quit or were fired from previous jobs (which can make or break your chances of getting hired)

The primary benefit of using this process is you'll find a permanent solution to your job frustration, instead of bouncing from one unfulfilling position to the next. You'll have a better idea of what's going to satisfy you. That results in smarter choices and commitment to those choices, which ultimately leads to success.

If you're presently feeling that events at work are pushing you toward resignation, this book will help you step back from your anger, frustration, and anxiety so you can examine your career and make a transition for the better. The end of one job should lead to the beginning of a better experience. Each move should help you grow and achieve more of what you want from your work life.

It is said that the mark of good pilots is not how well they take off but how skilled they are at landing. We hope the techniques presented in this book will help you make a smooth landing in whatever manner you choose to resolve your problems.

PART ONE

Coming to Grips with Your Job Frustration

1

Regaining Control of

Your Work Life

*There are times in everyone's life when something constructive is
born out of adversity. There are times when things seem so bad
that you've got to grab your fate by the shoulders and shake it.*

—Lee Iacocca, *Iacocca*

IF you've reached the point where you're seriously considering quitting, you may find yourself on an emotional roller coaster, alternating between apathy and rage. Often the overriding feeling is one of frustration, of being stuck in an unpleasant or unsatisfying position and being powerless to do anything about it. You're feeling pushed around by events and the people who dominate your environment; the job is controlling you. In this situation, there is a tendency to contemplate one of two options: quit on the spot the next time you're under duress, or take the first job that's available.

The first step, then, before your emotions get the best of you, is to regain control. This begins with reshaping your attitude and redirecting your energy into positive action. Rather than dwell on matters over which you have no power—company politics, an overbearing boss, or whatever your problems are—turn your focus toward what you *can* do to get ahead within your company or to get along better with your boss. You have the power to improve the situation or bail out, whichever is the best choice.

You're Only Powerless If You Choose to Be

Remind yourself that you chose your current job. You weren't sucked into it by some implacable force. And you are no more powerless to find a satisfying solution to your situation than you were powerless to get the job.

It's easy to lose perspective, because one's immediate supervisor and those above him or her wield so much authority. They have the power to give or withhold choice assignments, territories, promotions, raises, and so on. These people often attain Olympian status in the minds of their employees.

One small company I'm familiar with is run by an autocratic, demanding, and egotistical chief executive officer. The employees actually refer to him as "god," and it's only half-jokingly. He has a way of making his employees feel every major task they undertake is a life-or-death situation. It's every effective. A former employee admitted to me that, "Looking back, I can't understand why I felt so totally dominated by that guy; why I let someone so petty and wrong-headed erode my confidence and self-esteem!"

People often realize only after the fact that it's their own fears and anxieties that make their superiors larger than life. You can choose to let them get to you and propel you into an unplanned exit, or you can regain control and move forward in spite of them.

You Do Have Options

Accept it as a given that you have options. You may not see them now, but when you begin searching for alternatives with an open mind, you will find them. This process often involves a considerable investment of time and energy. And there may be difficult choices. But ultimately, you'll begin moving down a path that will lead to greater job satisfaction.

Who could have felt more doomed than a geologist in the oil downturn of the mid-eighties? Hal had risen to a middle-management level at a major international oil company and knew it was just a matter of time before his job was eliminated along with several hundred others. He felt defeated, thinking it would be impossible for him to match his rank and salary anyplace else.

He was frustrated and angry when he first talked about the bleak outlook for his career, fearing that his family's standard of living and his self-esteem were about to plummet. Then we discussed how his skills could be transferred to other administrative jobs. One option we explored was banking—his familiarity with the oil business and financial risks gave him insights that few loan officers could match. Eventually, Hal took a management position in the oil and gas department of a large bank, at a salary that was close to what he'd been earning.

Focus on the Positive

Hal's transition was a success because he managed to get beyond the emotional barrier that paralyzes people in such difficult situations. Anger and a deep sense of frustration are typical by-products of a job gone sour. They create a double-edged sword. To a point, these emotions will energize you and push you toward taking action. But if you fail to channel these emotions constructively and only dwell on what you can't control, these strong feelings will work against you.

To prevent these emotions from getting the best of you, concentrate on what you *can* control rather than what you are powerless to change. Russ, a former sportscaster at a midsize Florida television station, offers a good example of taking charge.

From the time he was five years old, Russ wanted to be on television. He worked his way up to become a sports anchor by the time he was twenty-five. For the first year, he relished the contact with sports stars and high visibility in the community. Then the glamour started to fade. He couldn't believe such an exciting job could become so routine.

By his twenty-seventh birthday, he was actually questioning whether he wanted to be an on-the-air personality for the rest of his life. "I couldn't see myself at age forty-five saying, 'The Mets beat the Cardinals four to two,' " he said.

That realization was deeply distressing and frustrating to Russ. He had been totally dedicated to establishing himself in a very competitive field, and now it appeared he was going to have to start the process all over again, doing something else. "To give up what I had was like giving up everything I had ever worked for—my whole identity," he said.

But rather than let the prospect of a difficult transition immobilize him, Russ started exploring his options. He'd always had an interest in business and he thought about going back to school for his M.B.A. To be sure he was making the right decision, he tested the waters by taking an accounting class, knowing that if he could get through that notoriously tedious course, he could get through anything. His high marks convinced him that he was a candidate for graduate school. Friends advised him to apply at the top five business schools in the country. He did and was accepted at his alma mater—Columbia University.

At first he was unsure about returning to New York City because he preferred the warm Florida climate. Yet he made the move, got his degree, and was hired at CBS-TV after serving an internship. While being interviewed for the job, managers who perceived the on-camera side of the business to be more fun than the behind-the-scenes work kept asking why he left sportscasting. "It was hard to convince people that I wasn't crazy," he said. But what he learned from broadcasting has helped him considerably in the business department.

Russ was successful in moving to a different job in the same industry because of the way he approached and carried out his decision. He turned his frustration into action. He weighed his alternatives very carefully, then executed the option he chose in a methodical manner. The whole process took a few years, which isn't unusual for someone who is making a major career change. On the average, people spend twelve to eighteen months making this type of transition.[1]

Give Yourself Time

Russ's example also demonstrates another critical requirement for controlling your destiny: time. Give yourself plenty of time to sort things out and implement a plan. While the idea of extending your stay at work may seem excruciating, you'll find that, once you begin this process, some of the sting will go out of your job because you're focusing on the positive, taking constructive action, and searching for a solution.

Be Open to Transition

If the process of undertaking a job or career shift seems intimidating, it's only natural. Transitions are scary. Luis Martin is the first to admit it. Few things are more traumatic than adapting to another culture and a foreign language, but the Spanish-born professor has done it twice —in Japan and in the United States. In both cases, he adapted well enough to be recognized by each nation as an outstanding educator. But perhaps his most arduous transition was leaving the Jesuit order after twenty years.

"I cannot possibly tell you one or two or three specific reasons why I made that decision," said Martin, who now holds a history chair at Southern Methodist University. "I think it was much more, really a long period of change, of transforming yourself, of realizing that the things that caused you to do something fifteen years before did not make any sense anymore."

He believes that being open to change is the essence of living a full life and one of the most important lessons of history. "To acquire a sense of yourself and at the same time realize that living is leaving behind, moving forward," he says. "It's scary. It's one of the scariest things."

He urges people to "face the challenges of a new reality, not with fear, not with shrinking back into the womb or your job or your culture or your language, but with a sense of exhilaration that you have been chosen to explore a new reality."[2]

Getting Control: A Frame of Mind

Resolving an unhappy work situation starts with a frame of mind that allows you to begin seeking the solution. Permit yourself to consider, as unlikely as it may seem now, that all of this unpleasantness may provide an opportunity for you to find something better. What's required is that you remain open to options and that you have the courage to follow through on them.

The courage to act stems from the confidence that what you are about to undertake is the best choice for you. That certitude comes from knowing yourself and clearly understanding why your present situation is not working out, which is the next step toward resolving your job problems.

2

Understanding the Source of

Your Job Dissatisfaction

Man, ignorant of self, creates his own unhappiness. The world masters him, when he was born to master the world.

—Paul Brunton, *The Secret Path*

WHY do you want to quit?

That may seem like a simple question, but if you sat down right now and made a list of all the things that upset you about your job, there's a good chance you would only be identifying the symptoms of your discomfort, not the real cause. Frequently, the true source of your unhappiness lies buried beneath these irritations.

For instance, Marge was frustrated by the problems she encountered while working with three co-workers in developing a chain restaurant's training programs. All four of them had different personalities, work styles, and objectives.

Marge's initial comments, which dealt with the friction between her and her co-workers, might have indicated that she needed to work with a different set of people. But as Marge discussed her personal and work history, it became apparent that she preferred more autonomy and direct control over projects. She talked about being an only child who was accustomed to spending time by herself. Although she got along well with most people, she had difficulty working in a team situation because she was used to making her own decisions and acting on them as she saw fit. The solution in her case was to transfer to another department where she could work more independently.

The Obvious and Not-So-Obvious Sources of Job Dissatisfaction

Not all job problems are created by something festering below the surface. Issues such as inadequate pay, no opportunity for advancement, too many hours, too much travel, etc., are generally clear-cut. Your dissatisfaction may be completely attributable to such obvious sources.

At the same time there are instances, as in Marge's case, when what is obvious is only part of the problem. Many times the only way to get to the heart of the matter is to stand back and examine your situation through careful, methodical self-evaluation. You must not only look at *how* you react to certain work situations and people but *why*.

Even if you're confident that you know what's causing your suffering, going through this introspective process is a useful exercise. Socrates proclaimed that the highest wisdom is to "know thyself," and there is no better advice that I can give my clients. Psychological studies have shown that people who have a greater self-awareness—a true sense of their strengths and weaknesses—are better able to manage their lives.

At a minimum, this self-examination will reaffirm that you clearly understand yourself and your needs, which will strengthen your confidence when it's time to act. On the other hand, it may reveal that there is more going on than you ever imagined.

Getting to the Source

It's no simple task to examine the often complex circumstances that lead to employment-related problems. There are, however, some basic techniques that will help you gain a better understanding of why you are experiencing difficulties.

Begin by relaxing and clearing your mind of anger, frustration, and other strong emotions that may prevent you from looking at your situation clearly and objectively. I suggest you take this book and a pen and find a quiet comfortable place to relax.

This will help you prepare to list *all* of the things at work that are bothering you. Don't edit your thoughts; just let them flow. To help you examine each aspect of your job, look over the list of job conditions below and ask yourself, "If I could change anything about this, what would it be?"

Basic job conditions: physical surroundings, ambiance, size of office, comfort and safety, etc.

Work schedule: number of hours required, flexibility

Location of job: city where job is located, distance from home, etc.

Amount of stress or demands

Pay and benefits

Opportunity to use abilities and pursue interests

Relationship with boss

Relationship with co-workers

Opportunity to pursue meaningful and challenging work

Responsibility and power

Rewards and recognition

Opportunities for professional growth

Job security

Economic outlook

Impact on personal life

Other concerns

Now go back and look at each comment. Put a check by the concerns that have the most profound impact on your happiness, such as a bad relationship with your boss, overwork that could lead to job burnout, being stuck in a position with no advancement opportunities.

Less significant concerns would include such complaints as your office being too small or an individual at work who's difficult to work with but who doesn't seriously impede your job performance. These are matters that are unpleasant but not serious enough to make you resign. They may, however, be the symptom of a much more serious matter. Being unhappy with the size of your office may be an indication that you feel unappreciated.

Look at the major issues and ask yourself why this situation is upsetting you, or why things aren't working out. Jot down your ideas after each complaint. Attempt to get to the bottom of each problem as best you can. Only when you identify the source can you devise a solution to the problem.

Be as specific as you can. Remember that a response such as "I'm unhappy with my job because I'm bored" is not getting to the source. Being "bored" is a symptom of the real problem. You must identify what's causing your boredom. Is it that your work offers no challenge or lacks contact with people or requires a tedious approval process?

Looking at Future Possibilities

Next, take a look into the future. Is your present job bringing you closer to your long-term career goals? Do you think you'll want to be in your current occupation five to ten years from now or for the remainder of your work life? Are you feeling a pull toward something else?

This is an important consideration. It will be discussed in more detail when you draw up the Career/Life Plan outlined in chapter 6. You may have some general ideas about where you would like to be in the future. If your current job doesn't fit into this master plan, you could be

What To Do About Sexual Harassment

First, confront the person and say that you're offended by the behavior and it has to stop. If the harassment continues, write down details of what happens and report it. If a co-worker is causing the problem, tell your boss. If it's your boss, go to his or her supervisor and discuss the matter.

The offender is likely to bother others if you don't blow the whistle. Around 20 to 30 percent of working women have been put in this uncomfortable position.[1] And now there are more and more complaints from men who have been harassed by women and from individuals who have received advances from the same sex.

These complaints have often led to an offender's dismissal or transfer. But if nothing is done and this harassing person makes your work life more difficult, consider filing a civil suit against the individual and, if it's warranted, your company.

headed for trouble. Jot down any factors that may be preventing you from moving closer to your goals.

Work/Life Themes

Look back on your past work and personal experiences. This portion of the exploration can be the most revealing. Its purpose is to identify work/life themes—patterns of success and failure in your career and personal life that will help you determine where you belong in the workplace and what you may need to change in yourself.

To help you get a firm handle on how this process works, we'll take a look at case studies in which individuals learned

15

to identify work/life themes while resolving two of the most common job problems: incompatibility with a job or career, and conflicting relationships with a supervisor or colleague.

Job Incompatibility

Two-thirds of all American employees are in the wrong job, according to studies by People Management, a consulting firm in Simsbury, Connecticut.[2] Many people make career choices before they really understand themselves. Their destinies are shaped to a large degree by external influences and pressures, such as parents, friends, and trends.

Parents often play a powerful role in shaping your behavior on the job, even if you've disregarded their plans for your career. Over the years, your parents have passed on their attitudes about their own jobs in both direct and indirect ways. Think back on the comments they made about work and the major events in their careers which made an impression on you.

Spouses, too, can shape your goals and expectations in profound ways. The success of siblings and close friends can also seduce you into trying to measure up to them on their terms, keeping you locked in a career or at a particular job that isn't right for you.

All these external pressures and stimuli tend to throw a fog over the career path that's best for you. As a result, some people get started off in the wrong field entirely. Others begin in the right field, but in a job that doesn't make the best use of their talents. And a sizable number of people assimilate attitudes toward work that are harmful to their careers.

As you read through the following case studies, you may

see some similarities to your own situation. The manner in which these individuals made discoveries may spark some creative thinking about how you can better understand the underlying reasons for your dissatisfaction.

Right Career, Wrong Job

The symptoms of job incompatibility don't always manifest themselves in the most obvious ways. It may appear that a person is in the wrong career or wrong company when actually there is another problem. For instance, Brad, a bright, capable engineer for a large aerospace manufacturer, procrastinated so much that the quality of his work had fallen significantly. He put off his own work by helping others with theirs. Eventually, his boss caught on and chided him for it.

As Brad talked to me about his background, it became apparent why his work performance had suffered. While growing up, his father's job transfers had forced the family to move frequently. Brad had attended six different schools before he graduated from high school. Unlike many children who resented this much uprooting, Brad adapted to the point that he looked forward to the next move; he liked the stimulation of change and prided himself in being able to adapt well to new surroundings.

When he took the job with the aerospace company after graduating from college, he did exceptional work for the first eighteen months. Then, as he settled into a routine, he became restless and bored. He wasn't accustomed to being in one place for so long and doing repetitive work. The only way he knew how to cope with the situation was to look around for something different to do, so he began helping others with new projects while letting his work slide.

The solution in Brad's case was to have a discussion with

his understanding boss and explain that he needed to find more challenging work. Eventually, Brad was transferred to another department where he could get the variety he relished. Fortunately, Brad was able to salvage his job after recognizing that he was in the right company and field but needed a position that fulfilled his need for stimulation.

Wrong Job, but What's Right?

In other cases, job incompatibility is obvious, yet knowing why and what options to choose are less clear.

Larry went through a rather lengthy career discovery process when he thought about quitting his job as a biomedical engineer in Palo Alto, California. To those around him, Larry appeared to be very successful. He made $60,000, drove a sports car, lived in a comfortable home, and was well respected at work. When someone had a tough question, they came to him for an answer.

But Larry grew more restless at having to comply with the company's rigid rules. "I know this sounds silly," he said, "but I finally became irritated at even the small things—like the time I was chastized for reading a magazine after I'd finished my work. I told my boss I didn't have anything to do, and you know what he suggested? That I reread the company manuals because it didn't look good for me to enjoy my magazine on their time."

Larry's weight ballooned to nearly three hundred pounds before he realized he had to take major steps to turn his life around. When he told his wife he was going to quit, she threatened to leave him, saying he was being irresponsible for walking away from such a well-paying job.

He agonized over whether he could give up everything—his work, his wife, and his life-style. In the process, he began looking at the source of his discontent and reevaluating what he wanted from life.

Larry reflected on his early years as the son of a marine sergeant who ran his household the same way he ran his military unit. Larry tried to be the perfect "little soldier" to please his father, but his independent nature made it difficult for him to take orders.

He preferred to have more control over his own life and enjoyed the challenges he experienced as a Green Beret medic in Vietnam. But once he got out of the service and began working at the laboratory, he had few outlets for his basic drives.

When Larry compared his successes with his failures, he saw how he tended to rebel against authority at work the same way he challenged his father's strict orders. Yet he thrived in situations where he could take charge. He was basically an entrepreneur at heart who needed to be his own boss.

Opportunities to do what he wanted were very limited in his job, so he quit and accepted a friend's offer to sell insurance. He hoped this temporary job would placate his wife, but she eventually filed for divorce. His parents were so alarmed by his behavior that they suggested he seek psychiatric counseling.

Despite these personal difficulties, Larry continued searching for a business venture until he was encouraged by another friend to begin selling limited partnerships on large tracts of commercial and industrial property. It's a risky business, but Larry has succeeded in negotiating major contracts.

"The money isn't as important as how I feel about myself," Larry says. "For the first time in years, I'm happy. My weight is back to normal and I'm optimistic about the future."

Larry could have made some unwise choices if he hadn't taken the time for soul-searching. If he had moved on to a different job in the same field, he might have experienced the same set of problems and perpetuated the cycle.

Rejecting the Right Career

Sometimes job dissatisfaction results from having turned your back on a career that you truly desired in order to chose something more practical or secure, which is what happened to J. B.

Originally, J. B. planned to use his theater degree and pursue acting, but then he got married, had a son, and decided he had to choose a more "responsible" profession. So he went back to school and studied engineering. For ten years, he worked at a succession of well-paying positions.

J. B. enjoyed the initial learning phase of a job and the challenge of doing something creative. But he couldn't cope with the day-to-day routine. "Designing door hinges for new systems wasn't my idea of living," he said.

He tried to improve his work life by making frequent changes. He changed homes, changed states, and finally changed wives. One year he had three different jobs and was fired from the last one because his apathy was so obvious. "I was actually relieved when they let me go because I didn't want to work there anyway," he said.

He finally admitted that he wasn't cut out to be an engineer. He was an actor at heart.

Pursuing a career in the theater meant giving up the financial security he had once known. At times he was tempted to turn back, but as he became better established and began getting steadier work, he felt more confident of his decision. "I'm happier now and more at peace with myself. When people hear my story they say, 'Gee, I really wish I had the guts to do that.' And I tell them, 'Well, why don't you? Get out there.'"

J. B. finally determined that the desire to pursue what he really wanted from life was stronger than his need for financial security. Many career choices involve giving up some benefits in order to get something that is more critical to long-term happiness. You have to be honest with yourself in determining your priorities and what is going to make you happy.

Work/Life Theme Self-Evaluation: Job Incompatibility

The following exercise is designed to help people who are in the wrong job or career, although these questions may be useful to anyone who is tempted to quit. Begin by thinking about the highlights of your present and previous jobs. Refresh your memory by looking at your updated résumé and thinking about all of your work experiences, from the time you had your first paying job to your present situation. Jot down your thoughts about the following questions:

What did you like about each job?

What did you dislike about each job?

What did you learn and what skills did you acquire?

21

What did you accomplish?

In what areas did you excel?

Where did you fall short?

What kind of supervisors did you get along with the best?

What kind of supervisors did you have difficulty tolerating?

What are the highlights of your personal life, including educational achievements (degrees, special projects, athletics, and extracurricular activities)?

What are your accomplishments in activities outside of work, such as projects you completed at home or involvement in professional, religious, civic, or volunteer organizations? (For example, if you did a superb job redecorating your home or if you were particularly proud of being recognized for your service as a volunteer in a local charity, include that.)

Go back over your lists and select the top five events of your professional and personal life. These include your biggest accomplishments and your most satisfying moments.

1. _____

2. _____

3. _____

4. _____

5. _____

Examine your top five events and identify what personal skills and conditions made things work for you. These would include such attributes as talents for organizing, creating, leading, getting along with others, following through on a project, etc. Make a note of how the environment, people, attitudes, and other elements contributed to your success.

1. _____

_____

2. _____

_____

3. _____

_____

4. _____

_____

5. _____

_____

You can learn a great deal about yourself by examining the personal skills and external factors that enabled you to enjoy your successes. Do you see a common theme in your work experiences? A repetitive pattern? For example, you may have excelled when you had an opportunity to work independently, lead a group project, think conceptually, or organize an event. Write down any repetitive themes you identified.

Because failures often teach some of life's most important lessons, go back and search for problems you've had in your work life. Some people encounter the same problems at each job. For instance, do you repeatedly have difficulty dealing with supervisors, or with certain skills or procedures? Jot down any negative repetitive themes you can spot, and consider why they may be occurring. In subsequent chapters, you'll look more closely at what you can do to eliminate these negatives.

What prompted you to quit jobs in the past? Make a list of the reasons. Have you repeatedly had the same reason for resigning? If so, it's especially important to understand why you quit in order to break a self-defeating cycle.

If you've made a career change in the past, what prompted you to switch fields? What roles have other people played in your career choices?

Identifying Positive and Negative Patterns

Review your work/life theme evaluation and complete the following statements. These responses will help you identify your greatest strengths and weaknesses. As you complete each statement, consider whether you're using your assets at your current job. Also, examine whether some of your weaknesses are contributing to your job problems.

Positive

My biggest successes occur when I'm using these skills:

I get most excited about doing a job when the goals involve:

I feel most comfortable and productive when the environment is:

I get along best with people who:

Negative

I consistently have difficulty or failures when I:

I'm least excited about doing a job when the goals involve:

I feel uncomfortable and unproductive when the environment is:

I have the most difficulty with people who:

Ideally, your job should give you an opportunity to use your strengths, interact with compatible people, and thrive in a stimulating environment. If any of these conditions are missing, you are bound to be dissatisfied. Your frustration may be compounded if your job includes any of the negative factors you listed.

Interpersonal Conflicts

About 60 percent of all job complaints center around business relationships, usually with supervisors.[3] Any number of factors affect the manner in which people get along in the workplace. If you're having difficulty working with your supervisor, that person may be a genuinely poor manager. Studies show that a high percentage of bosses are lacking in critical management skills.

But sometimes relationship problems can be exacerbated by the way you respond to an individual on an unconscious level. That person could be triggering bad feelings from past relationships or be causing you to unconsciously employ old defense mechanisms that are no longer appropriate. It's worth taking a little time to investigate why you feel the way you do when you interact with this person.

The "Inner Child"

In his highly regarded book *Leader Effectiveness Training,*
Dr. Thomas Gordon talks about the "inner child of the
past" in every employee. As children, we try out different
behaviors to cope with the various authority figures in our
lives. Those behaviors that work are used over and over;
they become our habitual responses to the adults who try
to control us.

As Dr. Gordon points out, these coping mechanisms are
seldom discarded when we pass into adulthood. They remain an integral part of our personalities, ready to be
consciously or unconsciously called up when we enter into
a relationship with an authority figure.

Most often, it's how we've learned to cope with family
members that has the most profound impact on our behavior at work. We spend so much time with people at the
office, they can soon seem like an extended family. The
roles co-workers play are similar to those in a family structure. Bosses have parentlike authority while co-workers are
on an equal level, much like siblings.

When difficulties with superiors develop, understanding
whether the problem lies mainly with your boss's behavior
or with your response to it will help you decide whether
it is appropriate to try to make changes in your environment or in yourself.

Michael, twenty-nine, discovered his "inner child" while
working in the marketing department of a major snack
food company. It was Michael's job to conceptualize marketing plans for new products. He was good at it, and he
liked his work. He also admired and respected his department manager, whose marketing skills were legendary.
The manager also had a way of generating infectious enthusiasm for each project. Yet Michael's manager also had

a notorious temper, and he would frequently explode at an employee whom he felt had fallen short of the task. No one escaped his wrath, including Michael.

During these dressing-downs, Michael found he was paralyzed. His mind froze when his manager angrily questioned him in a disorienting, rapid-fire manner, wanting to know why this happened, or such-and-such item was changed, or why things were delayed. Michael could just feel himself retreating inside. Later, alone in his office, he would think of answers to each question that justified his actions. He'd kick himself for letting his manager think that he'd dropped the ball.

Michael became more fearful of confrontations with his manager and began to grow angry and resentful. He was upset with himself for feeling impotent when confronted. He didn't want to leave his job, but he was finding it more difficult to cope with his boss's outbursts.

When we talked about these feelings, I asked Michael if anyone else in his life had that effect on him. After thinking for a moment, he said, "My father." Like his manager, Michael's father tended to verbally pounce on him in a rage. Michael learned early in life that when he tried to argue his case, it only further infuriated his father. So Michael would say nothing, believing it was the safest alternative, even when wrongly accused.

After examining past relationships, Michael was able to see how he had used that strategy in dealing with other authority figures. I encouraged Michael to remind himself the next time he was under attack and felt himself holding back that he was no longer a helpless child. He could defend himself and ignore the automatic response from the "inner child" and deal with his manager on an adult level.

It wasn't easy for Michael; patterns reinforced over the years are hard to overcome. Yet he made a conscientious effort and gradually reached the point that he was able to speak up to his manager when necessary. Thus, he kept a job that was very important to his career.

Parental relationships, of course, are not the only ones that have a profound effect on the way we relate to people as adults. Siblings, relatives, teachers, and others with whom we form significant relationships in our lives have helped shape certain automatic responses to both authority figures and peers in the workplace. Understanding these past relationships and how they affect your current situation can have a significant impact on improving job satisfaction.

Work/Life Theme Self-Evaluation: Interpersonal Conflicts

Your problems in dealing with certain work relationships should have surfaced in the work/life theme exercise you completed in the last section. If you're currently experiencing strained relationships with someone at work, take a few minutes to consider why you are at odds with and react to this person the way you do.

A self-analysis of work conflicts and possible resolutions is a bit trickier than the issue of job compatibility. If you're stumped by some of these questions, it may be to your advantage to talk to a counselor or therapist who can help you work out a strategy for dealing effectively with your situation.

Describe how the person you clash with at work makes you feel.

Have you had similar personal conflicts in the past? If so, describe the similarities and the person or persons with whom you had such conflicts.

Were the ways you dealt with these past relationships effective? What were the results?

What do you think you could do differently to work more effectively in this type of situation?

Put yourself in the other person's shoes and consider his or her responsibilities, demands, and pressures. Now look at yourself from the other person's point of view. You may find that some of your actions are contributing to the instability of the relationship. Could you make some adjustment in your behavior that would appease the other person without compromising yourself?

Even if you believe most of the problem lies with the other person, perhaps you could create a smoother working relationship by improving your communication skills

How Employers View Reasons for Quitting

Will employers consider your reason for quitting justifiable or will it make them think twice about hiring you? Based on our informal survey and discussions with employers, these are reasons that are considered justifiable.

- Better opportunity—the chance to advance or work for a more prestigious company.
- Higher salary—the opportunity for a significant increase in pay. As a rule of thumb, the raise should be a minimum of 10 percent and even higher if the job requires a move to another city.
- Additional education—taking time out to advance by increasing your knowledge in your field.
- More job security—the fear that your position may be eliminated because of a merger, reorganization, bankruptcy, or other difficulties.
- Starting your own business—cutting ties to be your own boss.
- Moving because your spouse is transferred.

Reasons that could cause concern include:

- Personality conflicts—being unable to get along with your boss or co-workers.
- Personal problems—a divorce, major illness in the family, or other difficulty.
- Work was too demanding—too many hours, too much stress, etc.
- Burnout—being worn down by job demands.
- Pursuing a fast-track career—frequent job-hopping to advance quickly.
- Protesting company policies—leaving with or without other employees to take a stand against unfair policies. If a lawsuit is filed, this action may also cause concern.

or simply learning to take that individual's behavior in stride. Remember that you'll run into difficult personalities no matter where you go. Strengthening your interpersonal skills and being sensitive to the needs of others can help you deal with problem relationships.

It's important to look at conflicts objectively, to recognize when you can deal more effectively with an individual and when your differences are so great that the relationship can't be significantly improved.

Good Career Decisions Spring from Self-Knowledge

The importance of self-knowledge cannot be stressed enough. It's the foundation upon which all important career decisions are based. Much can be learned on your own by using the techniques presented in this chapter.

Once you've completed this phase, you can approach the decision-making process of whether to leave your job or stay in it with a clear understanding of what conditions you require to thrive, what conditions don't suit your personality, and where you need to strengthen your skills to succeed in the job that's right for you.

PART TWO

CONSIDERING

WHAT WILL

MAKE YOU HAPPIER

3

Finding Your Job Niche

I hate my job. I hate my life. I'm going to Tahiti to paint.

—Paul Gauguin

U NLIKE Paul Gauguin, who left his dreary stockbroker's job for life as a painter on an island paradise, most people don't think broadly or boldly enough when considering job options. Yet it's a critical step in finding a satisfying job.

John Hunt, personnel manager of Southern California Edison in Rosemead, California, noted that many people are unsure of their job niche, particularly if they're changing industries. "I think a lot of people have great difficulty tying down in their own minds what they can do best versus what they like to do." When interviewing people for management positions, it sometimes becomes evident to him that an applicant really doesn't want to be a manager. Hunt believes these individuals are applying because they feel compelled to get into the managerial ranks to boost their careers or enjoy increased pay. "But it's evident in talking with a lot of them that their heart really lies in the technical aspects, not administrative, supervisory responsibilities."

You've probably met or read about people who've said, "I enjoy what I'm doing so much I can't believe they're paying me to do this." Chances are you're put off by this comment, thinking that *nobody* really loves what he is doing that much, or it's the good fortune of only a select few. Maybe you have the same belief as an acquaintance of ours who says people should just "find their rut and get in it," and not even delude themselves into thinking work can be enjoyable. But that's where you're wrong. We'll even go so far as to say it *should* be enjoyable. When you like what you're doing, commitment is automatic. Commitment fuels the kind of effort that breeds success. And succeeding is fun.

When Work Doesn't Seem Like Work

Trammell Crow, who founded and heads one of the nation's largest real estate development companies, is fond of saying that "work is more fun than fun." Robert Townsend, the guy who made Avis try harder, would tackle gargantuan corporate problems with the attitude of "having fun" in turning things around. Even our favorite waiter at a local Italian restaurant, a man who's done as much to build and maintain the restaurant's loyal following as its chef, talks about the "fun" he has serving and entertaining people.

Over and over again, we hear these kinds of comments from successful people. Are they just workaholics? No. The truth is, workaholics aren't really enjoying themselves. But people who are excited about what they're doing, who are passionate about their work, are the ones who are having fun. No one has fun all of the time, but it's perfectly reasonable to think you can find work that's enjoyable *most* of the time.

This chapter will give you an opportunity to think about work that will suit your personality, talents, and goals. It may be the same job you're in now with some improvements, or it could be a position in a totally different field. The main thing is that you'll consider numerous possibilities.

Listen to Your Inner Voice

Many people have some vague idea of what would make them happy, but every time they start dreaming of what they'd like to do, they dwell on obstacles. "I wish I'd gone into fashion design years ago, but at my age I'd feel silly going back to school." "My wife would probably walk out if I quit my full-time job and tried to make it as a consultant." "I'm too old to start a new career."

If you tend to shoot down your own dreams this way, you're refusing to listen to your "inner voice," that part of you that's trying to tell you what you really ought to be doing. No matter how difficult it might be to follow that voice and get on the right track, not doing it is eventually going to cause you more pain.

In recent years, studies have been done on the link between job dissatisfaction, and the low self-esteem and sense of helplessness that accompanies it, and the occurrence of crippling or terminal diseases. Feeling like a failure or even feeling mediocre at work has an insidious way of creeping into every aspect of our lives. Therefore, we urge you to say, "obstacles be damned," and do what you really long to do. As Bernie S. Siegel, M.D., put it so succinctly in *Love, Medicine & Miracles,* in which he persuasively explains the connection between job dissatisfaction and illness: "Take control of your life, find your true path, sing your song, and regardless of your age decide what you want to be when you grow up."

Adjusting Your Attitude for Success

Finding a job that will let you "sing your song" requires an attitude adjustment. You have to free yourself from thinking that you must be practical and only go after jobs that are readily available and easy to get. You also have to shake off any feelings of inadequacy that you may have as a result of your current situation. Below are some affirmations that will help you develop the attitude it takes to pursue the job that will make you happy.

I'm unique and have something special to offer. Your unique combination of talents and abilities allows you to make contributions at work that no one else can. You may have a special knack for dealing with people or be the one who always thinks of an innovative way to approach a problem. Whatever assets you bring to the workplace, use them. Find a position that allows you to maximize your strengths and minimize your weaknesses.

I'm willing to learn from success and failure. So much attention is focused on winning in our culture that many times people feel they are failures because they haven't had success in their chosen field or in a particular job. But failure is part of the long-term process of succeeding. If your current job is a disaster, at minimum you've learned what you shouldn't be doing. Many of history's most beloved figures, such as Abraham Lincoln, Winston Churchill, and Harry Truman, had a string of miserable failures before they found their niches and achieved success.

I'm not limited by my present job title. People box themselves into a corner by thinking of themselves in terms of their current job titles, limiting their options by considering only what they can do instead of what they want to do. But in the 1990s and beyond it will be impractical and even impossible for many people to cling to one career throughout their work lives. It's predicted that more than half of today's college graduates will end up working in a field that is different from their major.

Discovering Your Options

Discovering your options begins with a very general goal, which comes out of the strongest and most basic urge you feel in yourself, such as "I want to do something creative" or "I want to be a leader" or "I want to help people." Consider all of the ways you could fulfill that urge, keeping in mind that it doesn't have to be something for which you're currently trained. For instance, the desire to help people would give you a range of options that runs from being a police officer to being a psychiatrist.

One of the best ways to begin your search for options is to identify what you need in terms of six basic requirements:

- What you want to do
- Who you want to work with
- When you want to work
- Where you want to work
- How you want to work
- Why you want to work

As you consider these issues in the following exercise, we'd like you to relax, turn off your internal editor or judge, and let your imagination go. Even if you still feel that your options are limited, know that successful people *create* their choices by exploring every possibility. Think of options that you have never considered before. There's no need to decide what's practical and what's not at this point.

Conforming to old thought patterns can impede your progress. When Kevin went through this exercise, he became stuck because he couldn't think of any other way to use his business degree and his experience as an account executive at an ad agency. I asked him why he should restrict himself to something in business? After talking to him, I found that he had a passion for music, but he had earned a business degree because his father, a successful ad agency executive, had warned him that music was no way to make a living.

When I asked Kevin if he had pursued music at all since leaving school, he said that he'd done a few radio jingles to help out in a last-minute rush at his agency. Then we discussed the possibility of switching to the creative side of the business so that he could use his musical talents full time.

He decided to give it a try and volunteered to work on radio spots at his agency. Gradually, he built up a demo reel, which he eventually used to get a job at a music production house. Now he's composing music for everything from radio spots to feature films.

It's only by opening your mind to every viable option that you'll find your ideal job. The answers you give to the following questions will help you define your range of alternatives:

What do you want to do? What would you find most enjoyable? Most jobs can be classified according to whether they involve dealing with people, information, or things. There's a certain amount of overlap, but most jobs focus on one of the three. If you don't have a strong pull toward any one of these areas, looking back at your work/life themes will give you insights into your personal strengths. For instance, were your big moments involved in working alone and solving a problem, or were you playing a leadership role? Are you content to spend hours working with a computer, or do you prefer to interact with people and communicate your ideas?

Another way to open your mind is a dream exercise. Ask yourself, what is it I've always wanted to do? Whose job would I have if I could trade places with anyone?

With whom do you want to work? Consider how your personality, interests, and goals blend with those of others in a particular field. Finding the right job or career is somewhat like choosing a spouse. You won't be happy if you don't share some common ground with the people with whom you interact. Think about the personality types that dominate the jobs you find attractive. Consider not only people in the organization but also people you'd deal with on the job, such as clients and vendors.

When do you want to work? Consider the number of hours you're willing to work and the schedule. There's a trend toward more flexibility in work hours, allowing people to work as much or as little as they please. By the year 2000, 25 percent of all jobs will be either part-time, flextime, or contract, according to Tom Jackson, founder of The Employment Training Corporation (now Equinox Corporation).[1]

Do you prefer working regular, predictable hours or taking a job that may have a different schedule every week, depending on the work load? According to your personal biological time clock, do you prefer to start the workday early or do you like to get started later and even take projects home to finish at night? Think about the type of jobs that allow you to work during your peak performance hours.

Where do you want to work? Economic ups and downs make it important to think about what regions of the country offer the best job opportunities. A city with a thriving, diversified economy is an important consideration, especially for two-career couples who want to live where both can find satisfying work.

Not only should you consider where work is available, but where you'll find the climate, geography, and life-style that's most desirable to you. Also consider the type of office environment that would allow you to do your best work. Would you thrive in a large corporation where there are more resources and benefits, or a small business, where you might have a greater chance to make an impact?

How do you want to work? Are you looking for a fast-track job with high stress and an opportunity for advancement, or do you prefer something that's less demanding, making it easier to balance work with other interests? What kind of company fits your particular work style? Are you the type who likes to work in short, intense spurts, or do you relish tackling big, long-term projects?

For some, striking out and starting one's own business is the answer. This prospect has become more appealing to women. By the year 2000, half of the sole proprietorships in America will be owned by women, according to Susan Schiffer Stautberg, president of Master Media, New York.[2]

Why do you want to work? Forget the obvious answer that you work to make money and survive. That only satisfies our most basic needs. Work also serves as a means to satisfy our higher needs, or what Abraham Maslow calls self-actualization—achieving full potential as human beings. Most surveys indicate that people rate job satisfaction higher than monetary compensation. So think about what would really motivate you to get out of bed in the morning, then find an organization with the same goals in mind. Consider what type of work will be truly rewarding.

Brainstorming Alternatives

Go back and read through the notes you made in this exercise. Then begin thinking of jobs that would meet the needs you've identified.

You may want to browse through the *Occupational Outlook Handbook, Dictionary of Occupational Titles,* and other reference books in the library to identify some possibilities that you may not have considered.

If you find it difficult to get some ideas flowing, it may help to change your environment. Often getting out of town for a weekend helps you throw off limiting thought patterns and take a fresh look at your options. Even then, all of your best ideas may not surface at once. It takes time to develop options.

As you think about the jobs that would be suitable for you, jot down the alternatives below. List options that appeal to you, even though they may seem out of reach for one reason or another. You can list the jobs in a general way, such as "teaching at college level," or be specific about what and where, such as "teaching psychology at Stanford University."

_____

_____

_____

_____

_____

_____

_____

In chapter 5, you'll research your alternatives to determine which would be the most satisfying.

If any of your alternatives involves a career change, read the next chapter, which deals with moving into a different line of work. Otherwise, you can move ahead to part 3, the decision-making section, which will help you determine what's your best option and how it stacks up against your present job.

Do You Have What It Takes
to Start Your Own Business?

Before charging out to open up your own company, consider if you have what it takes to be your own boss. It's often more difficult than people think. Fewer than half of the entrepreneurs who start a business venture have a chance of succeeding.[3] Here are a few of the things that you will need.

- The drive to be a self-starter and the tenacity to last through the tough first years of a new business
- The ability to spot a special niche in the market that you can fill
- The skills to do well at your business
- The versatility to take over duties you may be unfamiliar with, such as marketing and accounting.
- Sufficient capital to get started and stay afloat until you can draw a salary
- Willingness to work long hours and do everything from ordering your company stationery to keeping business records to emptying the trash
- Willingness to learn and do everything you can to stay ahead of the competition

4

Changing Careers

When you're through changing, you're through.

—Will Rogers

DAVE Schleser had spent nineteen years as a dentist when he decided to trade fillings for fish. In his new career as an aquarist, or fish keeper, at the Dallas Aquarium, he couldn't be happier.

People wonder how he could take a cut in pay and prestige in exchange for planning fish diets and creating aquarium displays. Dave uses this analogy: "Say you go out to an expensive restaurant and spend a whole pile of money on a meal. When the food arrives, it tastes terrible. Why punish yourself by eating it?" In other words, why stick with something you don't like, just because you've got a lot invested in it?

Dave considers himself lucky in knowing what he wanted to do. From the time he was a small child, he had kept fish as a hobby. He was active in numerous aquarium organizations and met people in the field who encouraged him to join them. His work as a volunteer at the aquarium finally convinced him to sell his dental practice and make the transition.

Since then, he has talked to numerous people who are contemplating similar moves. "The big problem is that people don't know what else they want to do. Or they're not qualified for a different line of work and have to spend a long time in training," he said.

Signs That You Should Consider a Career Switch

You may identify with Dave and recognize your problems run much deeper than dissatisfaction over basic job conditions. The best move for you may be to change careers. Consider this possibility if you're experiencing the following:

- You are unhappy with the basic nature of your work.
- You aren't using your main abilities and skills.
- You have limited opportunities in your current field.
- You didn't want to enter this field in the first place, and only did so because of circumstances.

In a study conducted for the book *Successful Midlife Career Change*, Dr. Paula Robbins found that most people changed careers to find more meaningful work. The second most common reason for a career change was a better fit of values and work, and third was a chance for greater achievement. Money, material values, and status—commonly thought to be of primary concern to many Americans—ranked much lower.

This survey concurs with the findings in a Rand Corporation study on career change. Salary seems to be important in lower-paid occupations and meaningfulness and creativity are primary concerns in higher-level occupations.

Frequency of Career Changes

Today's workers will have an average of three different careers during their lifetimes.[1] And the frequency of switches is expected to increase in the coming decades. A large percentage of these switches will be made by people who'll recognize they're in the wrong field or they've outgrown it. Others will shift into a different career when they see opportunities diminishing in their industry.

There are four times in a person's life when a career shift is most likely to be made. The first period for many people is in their early twenties when they get their first hands-on experience in their chosen profession and find out they're unsuited. Another typical transition period is when workers reach their early thirties and see that change is necessary to meet their long-term personal and/or career goals.

The midlife change is the most talked-about period of reevaluation. This is when people reach a point where making a move is a now-or-never decision. Some move out of fields that are physically demanding, have limited financial opportunities, or are no longer challenging, and enter a profession that will be more rewarding as an older adult. Women may decide to seek more challenging work once they have fewer child-rearing responsibilities.

The final stage of change comes after retiring and starting another career that has fewer demands and is more compatible with a relaxed life-style. It may be a chance to pursue a dream job that has been postponed for many years, such as captaining a charter boat in the Caribbean.

What to Consider Before Making a Career Switch

Anyone who is preparing to make the big leap into another field must do his or her homework. Among the questions to ask are:

- Do I have a realistic idea of the demands and benefits?
- Will I feel comfortable in the new work setting?

- Do I have much in common with the people in this profession?
- What kind of training and education are necessary?
- Will I be able to meet the physical, emotional, and intellectual demands?
- Will the salary range be adequate for my needs five, ten, even fifteen years from now?
- What is the employment outlook for this field?

There are many initial adjustments to make, especially financially, because most people starting over in a new career can't expect to earn a salary that's comparable to what they've been making. And it may take time to acquire the education and training to prepare for something different.

Initially, many people suffer an identity crisis. There's often resistance to moving away from familiar people, job duties, and a way of life. To make it through the break-in period, remind yourself that the short-term unpleasantness is worth the long-term gain. You carry all of your past experience into a new field, and that's an important asset. If the career switch doesn't work out, you can always come back, which is what Sarah did.

After working for a major department store for several years, Sarah decided to open a small gift shop with her husband. They both had good business skills, and their mom-and-pop shop thrived. But after running her own business successfully for five years, Sarah found that the challenge was beginning to diminish. She enjoyed having control over her life but missed being in a position of power in a large organization and helping other people grow. She and her husband agreed that it was best for her to return to a retail chain. They found someone to take her place in the store, and Sarah landed a challenging job as an administrator in the finance department of a major store.

Tips for Successful Career Changes

When you get ready to make a career move, be sure the odds for success are in your favor. Here are some considerations to think about before putting your plan into action:

- Make a career change when you have few outside distractions. If you are coping with major stresses in your life, such as a divorce, death of a family member or close friend, major illness, etc., wait until a more stable period.
- Allow adequate time to prepare for a career switch. Perhaps that means sticking it out longer at your present job until you've saved up enough money for the transition. You may need to acquire additional education and skills before you enter the new field.
- Be realistic about the satisfaction you will receive from your career change. There will be periods of doubt, but overall the new direction should "feel right."
- Consider trying out a new career before severing ties with your current job. Sample what the work is like by taking a part-time job, doing volunteer work, or enrolling in training courses. Perhaps you can spend time with someone engaged in this work to get a preview of a typical workday. If that's not possible, at least talk to two people who are doing the kind of job that you're targeting.

Successful career-changers are not afraid to take a few risks in their lives. They look at their options, figure out what needs to be done, then go for it. Rarely do they look back with regrets on what might have been.

PART THREE

DETERMINING

WHETHER TO QUIT

OR STAY

5

Considering Your Options

Occupational choice is a lifelong process of decision making in which the individual constantly seeks to find the optimal fit between career goals and the realities of the world of work.

—Eli Ginzberg

SUCCESSFUL people have a knack for being in the right place at the right time. But it's not merely happenstance, as they're constantly developing and working out new options for themselves. They seem to live by the saying: "The harder I work, the luckier I get."

You've started this process by indentifying alternatives to your present job. Now you'll explore these possibilities and determine which one is best for you. This section involves reading and talking to others to find out more about each job or field. While gathering information, continue to ask yourself: "Is this job a good fit for me? Will I really be happy?"

If you already have a definite option in mind, explore it as thoroughly as possible to confirm that you're on the right track. When considering several alternatives, research each one to determine which is most desirable.

Look at the job or field from many different angles. All too often people focus on one or two aspects that really appeal to them, such as a high salary or prestige, while they fail to consider other conditions that may make the position less suitable.

Jessica, a lawyer, decided to move from a small, ten-person firm to one with three hundred people so she could handle more challenging and prestigious cases. What she neglected to consider was the atmosphere, the work load, and the partners' personalities and operating philosophy. "It's the coldest place I've ever worked," Jessica lamented. "Nobody talks to anybody. And everyone is expected to put in ungodly hours—nights and weekends included. It doesn't seem like anyone has a life outside of work. They're a bunch of law nerds." As an outgoing person who valued a balanced life-style, she had no choice but to start plotting another switch.

To make sure you consider the many different aspects of a job or career, ask yourself the following questions.

- Will I find this work meaningful and rewarding?
- Am I qualified for this type of work? If not, how do I get the training and education to pursue what I want?
- What preparations do I need to make before applying for this job?
- Will the pay and benefits be satisfactory?
- Will I feel comfortable in the work environment?
- Does this job allow me to live in a desirable location?
- Does this work offer satisfactory advancement opportunities?
- Can I cope with the stress from this work?
- How will this job fit in with family demands and outside interests?
- Will my family support this career decision? If not, how will I deal with potential conflicts?

- What is the economic outlook, considering changes in the industry, world market, technology, etc.?
- Where will this job lead?

Is It Time for a Sabbatical?

Do you feel like you're beyond job burnout? In that case, a two-week vacation isn't nearly enough time to decompress and get recharged. You might consider taking off from your job—temporarily or permanently—and pursuing some lifelong dream such as traveling through Europe, finishing a master's degree, or writing a screenplay.

Many people fear that such an unconventional act might jeopardize their career. What will employers think when they see this gap in their employment history? But more often than not, the response is positive. One woman who put that fear aside, taking nine months off to travel in Europe and work on a kibbutz in Israel, said, "I found that prospective employers were *more* interested in me after this short break in my career. They thought that anyone who was gutsy enough to do this would be a motivated self-starter. And they were right."

Sources of Information

One of the best places to begin your research is at a public or university library with a well-stocked business section. Ask a librarian to recommend all sources of information that would assist your search.

If you're targeting a major corporation, a good place to start is the *Wall Street Journal Index*. It provides condensed information on management, financial status, and recent events. Larger libraries will have annual reports of major publicly held corporations on file. If not, you can request one from the company's public relations department.

Take special note if there have been any recent major changes, such as a merger, cutbacks, restructuring, or management shakeups, or if industry analysts are predicting any of these events in the near future. In general, what's the overall health of the company and the industry itself? It's not in your best interest to hook up with a company that's in turmoil.

Find out the names of the company's top executives, including the chief executive officer, president, chief financial officer, and other key players. Check the *Reader's Guide to Periodical Literature* to find articles about them. Reading about the personal style and philosophy of top executives can tell you a lot about how the company is run and give you a sense of what it's like to work for these people.

If you're researching a new field, check the library's collection of business publications, trade journals, professional organization magazines, and books that can give you background on the job and the field in general. For a job that involves a move to another city, read the newspapers, city magazine, chamber of commerce publications, and other resources to find out more about the location. Ask your librarian about the availability of computer searches to help you get the most complete, up-to-date information on your subject.

Look for other sources of information, such as universities and community colleges that have counseling centers open to students and nonstudents. Many of them keep books and information about local companies on file.

Professional organizations and trade associations often provide an abundance of information about a particular career. *The Encyclopedia of Associations,* which is available at most libraries, has an extensive list of these groups. By tracking down the national headquarters, you can find the location of the nearest chapter, then attend a meeting or telephone a member to discuss job prospects.

What to Look for in an Annual Report and 10-K

Many annual reports contain a lot of hyperbole, but if you read carefully, you'll find out just how well a corporation is doing. Carefully skim the entire report, as the most revealing information may be toward the back, where you'll find a brief mention of a major quarterly loss or some other significant fact. Some annual reports have a ten-year summary, which is useful in determining trends, sales consistency, and earnings outlook. If this information isn't available, get the company's last three annual reports to make a comparison of profits, earnings, dividends, and shareholders' equity.

The shareholders' letters and management discussions may be a clue to how company leaders plan to approach the next couple of years. Statements about forming a new subsidiary or opening branch offices in other parts of the country could mean job openings.

Look over the corporate leadership and see if there are any big changes in store. If the CEO is about to retire, there may be a big management shakeup right around the corner. A woman who wants to get ahead should see how many women are officers or directors in the company. If all the board members are men, it may be a sign that women aren't readily promoted.

The corporation's 10-K, the annual report the company sends to the Securities and Exchange Commission, may reveal more details about the ages, backgrounds, and compensation of officers and directors, the company's competitive position within the industry, and how the industry has fared in the economy.

Information Interviews

Don't hesitate to contact people you already know in the field or ask for referrals from friends. Call sources at a time when they'll be most receptive—perhaps after work or when you know they're not too busy—and say that you'd like five minutes of their time to ask them a few questions.

Most people are willing to take a few minutes to help someone with their job search—nearly everyone who's employed has had to go through the same struggle. These information interviews can be invaluable. Some of the questions that can help you find out more about the field are:

- What attracted you to this job?
- How did you get started in this field?
- What do you find most rewarding?
- What are some of the drawbacks?
- What skills and education are recommended?
- What is the salary range?
- What are the job prospects and the best ways to find them?
- Will this be a good job or field to be in five to ten years from now?
- Can you refer me to other sources of information?
- Who else should I talk to?

What Will Happen to This Job in the Future?

The prospects for a particular field may look great today, but what will happen five, ten, even twenty years from now? That's an important question to consider in today's rapidly changing marketplace. By keeping an eye on shifts in the economy, you'll know when to alter your career course. Seeking additional training or moving to another region may prevent you from getting stuck in a dying field or getting boxed into a corner because you're a specialist with too few options.

In just this past decade, the labor market has been turned upside down by several major developments. Merger mania

---

Job Prospects for the Next Decade

The U.S. Department of Labor has compiled a booklet entitled *Tomorrow's Jobs: Overview,* which presents the following projections for the job market in the year 2000:

- 42 percent increase in jobs for health professionals
- 46 percent increase in jobs for computer and mathematics specialists
- 32 percent increase in demand for engineers, architects, and surveyors
- 30 percent increase in marketing and sales positions
- 27 percent increase for work in retail and wholesale trades, including restaurants, grocery stores, department stores, and machinery and equipment distributors
- 26 percent increase in the finance, insurance, and real estate professions
- 18 percent increase in construction jobs
- 16 percent increase in positions for teachers, counselors, and librarians
- 9 percent increase in the government sector, especially at the state and local levels
- 9 percent increase of jobs in transportation, communications, and public utilities
- 4 percent decrease in manufacturing jobs
- 7 percent decrease in mining jobs
- 14 percent decrease in the agricultural field

---

has eliminated thousands of jobs, especially middle management and above. Baby boomers continue to fight fiercely for the limited managerial positions, while the sixteen- to twenty-four-year-olds find an abundance of entry-level opportunities.[1] By the year 2000, nearly four out of five jobs will be service jobs, such as banking, insurance, health care, education, data processing, and management consulting, according to *Tomorrow's Jobs: Overview*, prepared by the U.S. Department of Labor.

Knowing what to expect will help you consider the optimum place to be in the future. Obviously, you don't want to choose something solely because it's considered one of the hot fields of the future. It helps, however, to be aware of trends in order to maximize your opportunities.

Selecting Your Top Alternatives

Let's see how your alternatives stack up. Spaces are provided at right for sizing up your top three alternatives, although you needn't limit this exercise to three choices.

Some of the questions may be difficult to answer if you don't have a lot of specific information about a particular job. Either leave it blank or make your best guess about how well it would meet your basic needs.

The rating scale, which lists basic considerations, will help you personalize the process by adding items that you think are important. For example, if you want a job that gives you a chance to move into management, add that to the list. The questions should cover all of your primary needs so you'll have an accurate reading.

Considering Your Options

Rate the jobs according to the following scale:

4 Excellent: Meets all of my basic needs
3 Good: Meets most of my basic needs
2 Marginal: Barely satisfies my basic needs
1 Poor: Doesn't meet my basic needs

This Job Allows Me to:	Alternative 1	Alternative 2	Alternative 3
Pursue meaningful and satisfying work	___	___	___
Work with people I enjoy	___	___	___
Spend most of my time pursuing activities I enjoy	___	___	___
Have satisfactory working conditions	___	___	___
Have a satisfactory work schedule	___	___	___
Work in a desirable location	___	___	___
Pursue a job that fits my goals and values	___	___	___
Have a satisfactory level of responsibility	___	___	___
Earn a satisfactory income	___	___	___
Maintain a balance between work and personal activities	___	___	___
(Add additional conditions that are important to you.)			
_____	___	___	___
_____	___	___	___
_____	___	___	___
Total points	___	___	___

Evaluation of Job Alternatives

Look at the difference in ratings. If one alternative is rated at least five points higher than the others, you have a clear preference for this job. Also check how you rated each consideration. At least seven of the items should be judged good or excellent. If you rated conditions lower than that, consider whether you can live with these drawbacks. If all three options have several marginal and poor ratings, repeat the research process to develop new alternatives.

Once you've selected a top choice, move on to the next chapter, where you'll determine how the job fits in with your career/life plan.

6

Drawing Up a Career/Life Plan

I learned at least this by my experiments. That if one advances confidently in the direction of his dreams, and endeavors to live the life which he has imagined, he will meet with a success unexpected in common hours.

—Henry David Thoreau

WHO would have guessed that a former Mr. Olympia, an Austrian with a tongue-twisting name, would one day become one of America's most popular film stars? Nobody except Arnold Schwarzenegger himself, because he knows how to visualize where he wants to be and to create a plan to get there.

As a teenager, Schwarzenegger became fascinated with the spate of Hercules movies that came out in the sixties. He began collecting muscle magazines, even hanging pin-ups of musclemen on his bedroom walls. "Within a year," said Arnold, "I had a very clear vision of where I wanted to go."[1] He went on to win the Mr. World title once, the Mr. Universe title five times, and Mr. Olympia seven times. His muscles provided his entree into the film world, where he's been building his acting career with the same creative visualization and discipline that he used to build his spectacular body.

Knowing where you're going in a career makes it easier

to make the right moves and maintain your momentum, even when things get rough. As you focus on what you ultimately want in a career, the right choice will become clearer when you decide whether to quit or keep your job.

Most people have a basic game plan in mind, but it's usually sketchy. A poorly defined plan tends to scatter your energy, and prevents you from zeroing in on your target —you may either aim too high or too low. At the end of this chapter, you'll fill in a career/life plan chart for stating your major objectives and how you'll achieve them. This process stimulates you to think of how to reach your goals in a logical, feasible manner.

We call the chart a "career/life plan" because you'll not only look at what's important to you on the job but your goals outside of work as well. You can't separate the two; one has an impact on the other. By considering all of your needs, a balance between work and the time you spend with family, friends, and outside activities may be achieved.

This career/life plan also will help you set short-term and long-term goals by determining where you'd like to be one to five years from now, as well as your ultimate goal. What you choose today will influence everything that happens in the future.

Payoffs in Career/Life Planning

Several employee-oriented companies have initiated different forms of career-planning. An international oil company, for example, asks employees to set goals and discuss them during their annual review.

Beverly, a twenty-eight-year-old corporate communications manager, talked about how much she gained from the practice. It not only helped her clarify her goals, it gave her boss a clearer picture of what she wanted.

"I wouldn't have been able to get this far without this

program," she said. "I told my boss several years ago I wanted to move into management. He gave me the chance to take on extra responsibility and eventually a new job overseeing internal and external communications was created for me."

Career/life planning also can help you:

- Be more aware of how to maximize your assets. You'll find more ways to use your talents and minimize your weaknesses.
- Remain in control of your life, so you won't be overly influenced by other people's demands, or allow them to make important decisions for you.
- Be confident that you can finish what you start. With a plan, you're less likely to be overwhelmed by the work it will take to reach your destination.
- Feel more committed to take action. Once you see what needs to be done, you'll be motivated to get started.

Different Types of Career/Life Plans

No two career/life plans are alike. The chart you'll fill out at the end of this chapter will reflect your uniqueness. You do have special assets that no other person has, assets that you can use to enhance future opportunities.

While mapping out your plan of action, consider how to get from point A to point B. It's helpful to understand your basic career management style, or career pattern. Here are five of the most common career patterns.

Lifer. These people are dedicated to one field, such as medicine, the arts, or science, and plan to stick with it for a lifetime. They prefer to acquire in-depth knowledge and continue to grow and expand their expertise in their chosen profession.

Ladder-climber. This group follows the traditional course of starting in an entry-level job and working hard to advance to the top of an organization. These people measure success by job title, salary, number of people supervised, and the size of their office. They are willing to make considerable personal sacrifices in order to be major contributors to the company's success.

Floater. To floaters, a job is secondary to their outside pursuits of happiness, hobbies, family needs, etc. They do whatever needs to be done, but are unlikely to be hard driving or eager to take on more responsibility. They value a congenial work atmosphere, job security, and few demands.

Adventurer. Adventurers aren't afraid to move from career to career. They're the risk takers. Once they have accomplished what they set out to do in one field, they welcome the challenge of starting something new. This group needs lots of stimulation, an opportunity to be on the cutting edge, and a chance to be in control of their own destinies.

Job-hopper. These people make more frequent job changes than the adventurer and have different motives. They're on a fast track to get ahead and hope that frequent job changes will help them move forward quickly. This group tends to be ambitious, independent, and sometimes rather impulsive when it comes to doing whatever it takes to get what they want.

Career Cycles

Another key factor to keep in mind is that your career/life plan will undergo many changes according to your age, family responsibilities, and priorities at various stages in life. That's why it will be helpful to update your career/life plan every couple of years or when you face major decisions. It's also necessary to understand the ebb and flow of career cycles to be prepared for different phases of your work life.

In their twenties, most people try out a chosen career to see how they like it and learn whether their skills and talents are ample enough to compete in that field. They're often willing to devote considerable energy and time to get ahead during their twenties, and into their thirties, hoping to be rewarded for their efforts.

People hit their prime in their forties and expect hard work to pay off. They also begin looking at how much time is left to achieve their goals.

In their fifties and sixties, people begin to reap the rewards of their success. Some begin winding down and preparing for retirement, while others make plans to launch a final career.

Men and women often go through career cycles at different times depending on family demands. Men may devote more energy to work during their twenties and thirties but slack off in their forties to spend more time with their families.

If women have children in their twenties and thirties, they often make adjustments in their career to care for young children. By the time these women reach their forties and fifties, however, they may devote more time to work than their husbands do because family obligations have diminished and women are eager to finally make their career mark.

As we move through these cycles, ups and downs will certainly be encountered. Knowing to expect "growing pains" will make it easier to move from one stage to another. Periods of shifting goals, changing priorities, disillusionment, and questioning are bound to occur.

As Gail Sheehy noted in *Passages*, "We are not unlike a

particularly hardy crustacean. . . . With each passage from one stage of human growth to the next we, too, must shed a protective structure. . . . Coming out of each passage, we enter a longer and more stable period in which we can expect relative tranquility and a sense of equilibrium regained."

Drawing Up a Career/Life Plan

Carefully consider your goals for each of the items listed on the chart at right, and ask yourself, "What's really going to be right for me?" Be as objective as you can.

Fill in the chart according to your short-term goals— what you want to achieve in one to five years. Then look at your long-term objectives. Some people will have a clear picture of their ultimate goal. Others who have difficulty imagining what they might be doing decades from now should focus on where they'd like to be in ten years or so. Be as specific as possible.

Next to the goals is a column for you to jot down how you'll accomplish each one. For example, someone who wants to advance from an entry-level position to take on more responsibility might accomplish this short-term goal by improving skills and working out a plan with the boss for gradually assuming more responsibility.

Because of unknown factors, most people won't be able to fill in all the "hows." But at least the statements will help you think about your future. Use the career/life plan chart on the following page to provide information about:

- Type of work—career, field, or specific company
- Title or rank—job title or description of the position
- Location—city, region, or country where you would like to live
- Income—amount of money you want to make

CAREER/LIFE PLAN

	Short-Term Plans	How to Accomplish	Long-Term Plans	How to Accomplish
Type of work				
Title or rank				
Location				
Income				
Personal goals outside of work				
Family plans				

- Personal goals outside of work—plans for activities apart from work, such as seeking additional education, becoming involved in professional organizations and community groups, or pursuing other interests
- Family plans—major events, such as getting married, having children, or taking care of elderly parents

Look over the career/life plan and consider whether your present job will help you reach your short-term and long-term goals. If not, will your alternative lead you there? This chart will indicate whether your job is actually helping you advance in the proper direction, or if it is locking you into a holding pattern.

7

How to Make the Final Decision

about Quitting

The difficulty in life is the choice.

—George Moore,
The Bending of the Bough

NOW that you've carefully assessed your primary option, you face what is often the most difficult part of the decision-making process—determining whether to keep or quit your job.

Every decision—from choosing a college major to selecting a spouse—involves risks that can paralyze action. But you will minimize stress and the chance of making the wrong choice by using a systematic approach to decision making. Research indicates that people who use a planned approach are more likely to stay committed and are less likely to have regrets afterward.

It's Your Choice

When a decision is particularly tough, there may be a tendency to rely heavily on a spouse, parent, or a trusted friend for a solution. In many cases, seeking outside opinions is advisable. But don't fall back on the excuse that you're making a choice because another individual persuaded or pressured you into doing it. If you don't feel responsible for your choice, you won't feel committed to following through with your plans, which will inevitably lead to failure.

Stay Positive

In the first chapter of this book, we stated that the way to get control of your situation was to approach decisions from a positive perspective. That advice is just as applicable now that you have reached the most critical juncture.

Dwelling on negatives—the risks of a job—can scare you into making the safest, but not the best, move. Risks certainly must be weighed, but they should not be the dominant consideration.

In *Career Satisfaction and Success: A Guide to Job Freedom,* Bernard Haldane suggests seeking the option that enables you to gain the most rather than looking at where you lose the least. By taking a more positive approach, you are apt to aim higher and be happier with the outcome than if you base your choices on the lesser of evils. "Most of us have been trained to relate to failure rather than to self-realization. The error factors in life can be used, as they are in satellites, as aids to a safe shift in direction" but not to dictate your destination, Haldane states.

The Decision-Making Model

Step One: Compare Job Conditions

In this first exercise, you'll rate the conditions at your present job and the conditions you expect to find at your alternate choice. Many aspects of each job will be considered, from basic rewards and opportunities to relationships with others and the long-term forecast for your field. This overview will help you weigh the most important considerations and provide a balanced picture of what both jobs offer.

When you look over the list of job conditions, there may be considerations to add for your particular situation. You may be thinking about switching jobs because you're about to be transferred to another state, so relocation should be added to your list.

As you complete the evaluation, refer to the following "Job Factors" section, which gives you specific points to consider. Keep in mind that if the desire to escape your current position is strong, you may have a tendency to overrate your alternative. Be as objective as possible to give a true assessment of what you're experiencing at work now, and what you expect to find at your alternative position. Use the point system to determine how well these factors satisfy your basic needs.

4 Excellent

3 Good

2 Fair

1 Poor

Job Factors	Present Job	Alternative
Meaningful and challenging work	___	___
Opportunity to use interests and abilities	___	___
Opportunity to meet career/life plan goals	___	___
Pay and benefits	___	___
Relationship with boss/supervisors	___	___
Relationship with co-workers/subordinates	___	___
Corporate identity and culture	___	___
Work environment	___	___
Location	___	___
Advancement opportunity	___	___
Level of job stress	___	___
Work schedule	___	___
Freedom and flexibility	___	___
Authority and responsibility	___	___
Status and recognition	___	___
Opportunity for professional growth	___	___
Job security	___	___

Economic outlook   ———   ———

Impact on personal life   ———   ———

Impact on others   ———   ———

(List other job factors that are important to you.)

Totals: ———   ———

Job Factors

Meaningful and challenging work
- Can you spend most of your time on important and worthwhile assignments?
- Is there a variety of quality assignments?
- Does this job foster professional growth?

Opportunity to use interests and abilities
- Do you have an opportunity to pursue what you enjoy the most?
- Can you use your greatest skills and talents?

Opportunity to meet career/life plan goals
- Does this job take care of your immediate and short-term professional/personal needs?
- Will this job help you attain long-term objectives for your professional/personal life?

Pay and benefits
- How does your salary compare with the industry average?

- Is the salary commensurate with your experience, education, and achievements?
- Will you be adequately compensated for all the hours you work, including overtime?
- What are the prospects for increasing your income?
- Are the benefits adequate based on your particular needs, age, and number of dependents?

Relationship with boss/supervisors

- Do you have compatible personalities?
- Do you have the same management/work style?
- Do you have similar values, goals, and ethics?

Relationship with co-workers/subordinates

- Do you have compatible personalities?
- Do you have the same work style?
- How do other employees affect the overall morale?

Corporate identity and culture

- Can you relate to the company's purpose and/or products?
- Does the company engage in social policies or practices to which you personally object (e.g., holding investments in South Africa, etc.)?

Work environment

- What is the basic atmosphere and ambiance like?
- Is your work space comfortable and well equipped?
- Does the company meet basic health and safety standards?

Location

- Is the job located in a desirable city?
- Is the job located in a desirable neighborhood within that city?

- Is the job easy to reach by personal or public transportation?

Advancement opportunity
  - What are the short-term and long-term opportunities for advancement?
  - What is the company's growth potential?
  - What is the company's policy toward promoting managers from within the company?
  - What is the company's record for upholding equal opportunity policies?

Level of job stress
  - Is sufficient time allotted to meet deadlines?
  - How demanding is management?
  - What type of crisis situations are encountered?
  - What is the likelihood of burnout or health problems?

Work schedule
  - How many hours are required per week?
  - What are the requirements for working on weekends, holidays, and split shifts?
  - How much time is given for vacations and holidays?

Freedom and flexibility
  - How much control do you have over what you do at work and when projects are finished?
  - Can you express your personal preferences in your dress and conduct?
  - Is flextime an option?

Authority and responsibility
  - Is there a gap between the responsibilities for which you are held accountable and the authority you have to carry out your job?

- Do you have many decision-making opportunities?
- How many people do you supervise?

Status and recognition

- Are you proud to be associated with this company?
- How do your peers, clients, and friends regard this job?
- Does this job measure up to your abilities and educational level?
- What type of feedback do you receive on your accomplishments?

Opportunity for professional growth

- Does this job allow you to become more knowledgeable and proficient in your field?
- Do you have an opportunity to acquire more skills through training programs or tuition reimbursement?

Job security

- What is the company's turnover rate?
- What are the prospects for cutbacks or mergers?
- Can your job be eliminated within the organization?

Economic outlook

- Is this position affected by local, national, or international economic conditions?
- Is the company keeping up with technological advances and other changes?

Impact on personal life

- Do you have enough time and energy to enjoy a balanced life-style and outside interests?
- How does this job affect your overall physical and mental health?

Impact on others
- How does your work schedule, including travel demands, affect your spouse, family, and friends?
- Is your family required to participate in numerous work-related social activities?

Rating job factors
Look over the basic job factors to make sure all of your primary concerns are covered. If not, add any others to the bottom of the list. Consider the basic factors at your present job and rate them in the first column. Then evaluate what you can expect to encounter at your alternative and mark a rating in the second column.

Evaluating job factor ratings
After tabulating the points, you'll see which job satisfies more of your needs. Here's how to interpret the scores:

- If your job alternative is at least ten points higher than your current position, you can improve your work life by moving on. Go back and look at how you rated your top five priorities. If there's a big difference in these ratings, you have an even clearer indication that you have more to gain at another job.
- A point spread of ten or more points in favor of your present job indicates you should stay and improve your situation. Perhaps your job-related problems are not insurmountable and you can find satisfaction if some changes are made. This rating may also indicate you have a weak alternative and should find a better job before quitting.
- It's often difficult to interpret a score that has less than a ten-point difference, as there's no strong indication that you have more to gain at one job or the other. Go back and look at how you rated your top five priorities. These are the make-it-or-break-it conditions that are most important, and in some cases, the ones that you know more about from the preliminary investigation you did on your alternative job. Add up the points in your top five priorities. See if there's an eight-point or more difference between your present job and your other choice. If

not, consider staying where you are and improving your job (tips on how to revitalize your job are given in chapter 8), or seeking a better alternative before making a switch.

Step Two: Imagine Commitment to Your Top Choice

An effective way to test the validity of your top choice is to picture what will happen to you in the future. If you remain in your present job, how will you carry out changes to revitalize your position? Or if you move on to another company, how will your life change?

Creating future scenarios is useful in decision making because it will help you think through a logical sequence of the events that can occur after you make a choice. Often it's beneficial to think of plausible scenarios for each alternative. Then try to imagine what will happen with the best possible outcome, the worst possible outcome, and the most likely outcome, which is usually somewhere in between.

In order to give you a better idea of how this works, we'll take a look at the choices one man faced and how he visualized the outcome of his decision.

Ross, twenty-eight, had managed a retail electronics store for five years. Originally, he had planned to become a computer sales representative after graduating from college with a degree in marketing and computer science. But he was sidetracked by the comfortable salary he earned working in retail.

Eventually, he got bored with his repetitive work routine and was afraid he would be stuck if he didn't make a move. After interviewing for several jobs, Ross was offered a position as a sales representative for a midsize computer manufacturer. His base pay would be lower than what he had been making, but he had the potential of receiving hefty commissions and bonuses if he was successful.

There was a mix of pros and cons involved in this new job. It offered him greater prestige and the potential for a more promising future, but he was not sure how well he would do in the competitive business-computer market.

A big drawback was moving three hundred miles away from his girlfriend, Jennie. They had been discussing marriage, but Jennie had a job she liked and strong ties to her hometown. She pressured him to turn down the computer company offer.

Ross wrestled with what to do. He was not totally dissatisfied with the job he had, but he felt a strong pull toward taking the sales job. To help clarify his decision, Ross rated the job factors and determined that more of his basic needs and requirements were satisfied in quitting and accepting the job offer.

Then he visualized where he would be a year from now if he took the job. He pictured himself wearing a casual shirt, shorts, and sandals, because his sales bonuses paid for a Hawaiian vacation.

Here's how he expected to respond to my questions:

COUNSELOR: It's been a year since I saw you. At that time you were thinking about changing jobs. I'd like to hear how things have gone over the past year.

ROSS: I went to work for the computer manufacturer. The competition in the computer market was just as tough as I thought. But I was prepared for it. I've learned a lot and I've done pretty well.

COUNSELOR: Are you satisfied with your decision?

ROSS: Yes, the move gave me a chance to get into a field I wanted to be in from the beginning, and I really like it. It's a lot more interesting than the electrical supplies and gadgets that I was selling before.

COUNSELOR: What about your personal life?

Ross: I had hoped to marry my girlfriend, but she won't leave town. She doesn't seem to be able to get away from her family or her job. We've had a lot of arguments lately.

Counselor: How do you plan to remedy that problem?

Ross: I've thought about compromises we can make. I could promise her that after we marry, I would move back to her hometown in two to three years. By that time, I'd be established in this field and might be able to get a job with another company. She could view her relocation as temporary.

Counselor: Considering the difficulties, are you still glad you made the decision?

Ross: I definitely made the right career move, and although my personal life is up in the air, I think that will work out eventually.

Creating scenarios

Now it's your turn. Pretend it's one year later. You decide to drop by a career counselor's office to discuss what has happened to you since you made your decision. Imagine how you feel about your job, yourself, and the concerns you have.

Try to respond to the questions below in as much detail as possible. When considering both good and bad situations, let your mind wander freely. Loosening up your imagination will inevitably uncover some considerations that you've overlooked or that have been lurking in your subconscious.

Don't be reluctant to visualize potential problems. Boldly examining these issues will not only assist the decision-making process but will prepare you to face these challenges should they actually arise.

The questions below are designed merely to get you started. If you have information about your job that will make more detailed questions useful, write them in. The more involved your internal dialogue is, the better. Use the model below to establish an ongoing dialogue in your mind with this imaginary counselor, allowing your thoughts to flow without inhibition.

COUNSELOR: When I saw you last year you were trying to decide whether to quit your job. What did you decide and how has that worked out for you?
CLIENT: During the past year, I decided to [quit/keep] my present job. Here is what happened when I [turned in my resignation/decided to salvage my job]:

After I made my decision, a lot began improving in my work life, such as:

COUNSELOR: You anticipated some problems when we discussed your choices. Did they materialize?
CLIENT: The major problems I encountered were:

COUNSELOR: Have you been able to resolve those problems?
CLIENT:

COUNSELOR: How has your decision affected your life outside of work?
CLIENT: The main impact has been:

COUNSELOR: Considering everything that has happened, are you still satisfied with your decision?
CLIENT:

Learning from scenarios

It's helpful to go through these questions several times and imagine different scenarios for quitting or staying. If you are successful in using this technique, some issues may surface that you didn't consider while rating job factors.

Look back at your responses, paying particular attention to issues that you didn't consider earlier, such as what happens after you turn in your resignation or decide to salvage your job. That will help you lay out a plan of action for carrying out the decision. If you see any roadblocks, they may affect your choice.

Also look at the problems you expect to encounter and

what will be necessary to remedy them. Be realistic about whether you can overcome the difficulties.

Picturing how your life outside of work will change helps you take a more holistic approach to job transitions. Because work affects all aspects of your life, it's important to consider how others will react to your decision and how your personal life may change. Add these findings—pro and con—to your evaluation as you complete the final step of the decision-making process.

Step Three: Make the Decision

In this final phase, you'll summarize your findings by comparing where you can gain the most and lose the least. This exercise will help you review what you have learned and see how the benefits of each choice balance with the drawbacks.

Review your job factor ratings and future scenarios to determine what's most important to you. Add anything else that you consider relevant.

Benjamin Franklin said that people cannot keep all the pros and cons in mind at one time. He advised writing down key points and considering them carefully.

As you ponder the pros and cons, consider how your present job and the alternatives allow you to:

- Regain control of your work life
- Resolve underlying job dissatisfaction
- Pursue the career that's right for you
- Feel more fulfilled and satisfied at work
- Feel more fulfilled and satisfied outside of work
- Achieve short-term and long-term career goals
- Achieve short-term and long-term personal goals

Final decision-making step

List the major benefits and drawbacks of each choice:

What do I have to gain by quitting my job?

What do I have to lose by quitting my job?

What do I have to gain by taking another job?

What do I have to lose by taking another job?

Unless your findings here are counter to what you discovered in steps one and two, the answer to the final question should now be quite clear:

Based on where I can gain the most and lose the least, my final decision is to _____

_____

_____

_____

Becoming Committed

The decision you just made won't mean much until you become committed to making improvements and changes in your life. When you commit, you accept the challenge to go for the best.

You should feel good after making the decision. If you have considerable reservations about either the method or the choice, you won't be ready to make a firm commitment.

Commitment happens in a series of small steps. Once you receive positive feedback on this particular choice, the readiness to act increases. Often these steps include telling family and close friends about the tentative decision. There will come a moment when the commitment is complete, such as when you sit down to write a resignation letter and think about what you will tell your boss about your decision.

If you're not fully committed to the decision, you may sound wishy-washy when you announce your plans to resign. Or you'll only halfheartedly pursue methods of improving your job.

The remainder of the book will help you carry out the decision. If you've chosen to stay in your job, you'll learn how to breathe new life into it and enhance the opportunities where you are. If you decided to quit, there are pointers on how to handle the numerous details in the resignation process, which are important in making a smooth transition to a better position.

PART FOUR

WHAT TO DO

AFTER YOU MAKE

YOUR DECISION

8

If You Decide to Stay:

How to Improve Your Work Life

A wise man will make more opportunities than he finds.

—Sir Francis Bacon

By deciding to stay, you've determined that your job still has a lot to offer, and that you can improve what you don't like. You've already progressed through an important stage, that of self-assessment and pinpointing what you don't like and where you want to go next. The next step is to come up with a solution to your job problems. It's important to remember that *you* will be the one who initiates the action that will lead to improvements. In most cases, you'll need the support of your boss, colleagues, and others to help you carry out your plans.

"Many times employees will complain about a situation, but won't have a solution or offer a compromise or resolution," said George Berger, human resources vice president at Tandy Corporation, Fort Worth, Texas. "If they intend to try and improve a situation, I think their first step is to decide what they want to accomplish, do their homework—develop a game plan—and then pursue it to a conclusion."

Here are three basic steps for planning a course of action to improve your job.

1. Consider the best way to make the change by brainstorming options on your own. Getting input from others who may have useful insights and/or have had similar experiences will also be helpful.
2. Begin taking action and evaluating the feedback to make sure your actions are having the desired effect. Make any adjustments that are necessary.
3. Evaluate your progress to see if you're accomplishing the original goal.

Many people find they're most successful if they work on improvements from the inside out. In other words, they look at changes they can make in themselves that will eliminate or reduce difficulties or conflicts at work. That could involve breaking old habits, such as procrastinating until the last minute and then panicking to meet deadlines. Then they move on to external, job-related factors that are getting them down.

Six Ways to Improve Your Work Life

1. Maintain a positive attitude

It may seem simplistic, but by feeling turned on and optimistic about the prospects of improving your job, you'll be in a much better position to make things better. People who feel disenchanted with their jobs have lost their sense of connection with work. They may ask themselves, "Why did I ever get into this type of work in the first place?" Rekindling the enthusiasm you once had will help you renew commitment to your job.

This self-motivation is particularly important if your colleagues are unhappy, because attitudes are contagious. And negative vibes seem to increase exponentially when you're surrounded by people who are as unsatisfied as you. The regular "bitch sessions" you and your co-workers may have can make it difficult for you to launch your improvement plan. Ultimately, you have to focus on the positive aspects of the job and not dwell on the negative issues.

2. Balance work and your personal life

While going through particularly trying times, you will find it easier to make internal changes by balancing work and your personal life. Seeking harmony between the two isn't always easy, especially when you're putting extra effort into improving your job.

"Realize that while work is important, it can't be the only thing in life for more than a limited time. Trying to make it such is a prime cause of burnout," says Glenn McClung, manager of Cooperative Personnel Services, a California consulting agency.

Take a tip from long-distance runners who learn to pace themselves. Set aside a time to work, a time for personal activities, and a time to relax. This will help you feel more rejuvenated when it's time to tackle your problems.

3. Increase your value as an employee

What can you do to become more proficient and respected in your organization? Most companies today are looking for people who can go beyond executing perfunctory tasks and come up with creative, innovative ways to solve problems, save money, and help organizations move ahead.

This challenge to an "intrepreneur"—one who works within an organization to create new and better ways of doing things—can provide the type of goals that makes work more stimulating. By looking for ways to go above

---

Has Your Career Reached a Plateau?

If you feel hopelessly trapped in the same, boring job, here are some ways to get noticed and move ahead:

- Look at how others have moved ahead in your company and do what it takes to get noticed, such as taking on extra assignments and learning everything you can about your job *and* the one you want.
- Get to know people in your company, not only in your department, but others as well. Look for natural ways to socialize through company-sponsored social events, intramural sports teams, and professional and civic organizations.
- Quietly promote your accomplishments by letting movers and shakers in your company know what you have done. Become a very visible member of your organization by contributing to the company newsletter, speaking up at meetings, and volunteering for high-profile assignments.

---

and beyond, you are more likely to receive positive feedback and rewards.

Effective approaches may include: requesting additional projects in an area that interests you, volunteering for cross-training in a related area, or developing a plan and presenting it with *you* as the coordinator.

Michelle began employing the first tactic six months after she went to work as a secretary at a video production company. Because competition for jobs in the industry is stiff, it's not unusual for young film-school graduates to start out in lower-level jobs. Michelle was promised that when something else opened up, she'd be given a shot at the job.

She proved in a short time that she was a good organizer, handled people well, and could learn quickly. Not willing to wait for a job opening, she volunteered to help write scripts when the staff writers were swamped and she filled in as a production assistant. Her boss noticed this extra effort, and she was promoted to assistant producer when business began to pick up. She eventually moved on to the position of producer, which was the job she wanted.

Think of ways to use your strengths to open up new opportunities for you at work. Then be honest about your weaknesses and see if there are ways to overcome them.

Some people have to break down their resistance to learning a new skill or trying a new approach. Lauren, a civil service administrator, recognized that part of her job frustration was tied in with her lack of experience using computers. At fifty-one, she resisted learning a few basic programs that could help her tremendously in doing quantitative analysis.

When she told her brother how exasperated she'd become, he offered a simple solution. He would be glad to meet her at the office on a Saturday and show her how to use the Lotus 1-2-3 program. They spent five hours together, and when they were through, she didn't feel so intimidated. She began practicing what she'd learned and trying out other software programs that helped her to work much more efficiently.

4. Improve difficult relationships

There are three ways to approach problem co-workers and supervisors: ignore the little things; compromise on less-serious differences; find solutions and discuss ways to correct major conflicts. Problems may exist because you have a totally different work style than your boss's. This individual may be a rigid Type A person who constantly hurries

Getting Paid What You're Worth

You can't depend on your company to automatically reward you for a job well done. When pay is a problem, it's time to begin lobbying for a raise. To prepare your case, consider what it takes to get noticed in your company and your industry. Some firms are especially impressed by people who are willing to go the extra mile and take on more responsibilities; others respond when employees begin dressing for success and actively promoting their accomplishments. Spend at least a month doing something special before you ask for a pay hike.

A good time to discuss an increase is during your annual review. But if that's too long to wait, arrange a meeting with your boss at a convenient time and come prepared to state your case for receiving a reasonable pay boost. Find out what other people in your position are making and use this information as leverage. Then bring up accomplishments, compliments, and other information that backs up the statement that you're worth more today than you were yesterday.

If your boss counters with a lower figure or says that the company can't afford this increase, say that you'd like to be considered for a promotion or extra duties to merit the boost in pay. Don't ever threaten to leave or start looking for another job. This initial meeting may result in a pay hike as soon as the boss can get it approved. If it doesn't, and you believe that you will be more adequately rewarded elsewhere, consider whether a job change is in order.

along projects while riding herd on you and the rest of the staff. You, on the other hand, may resent someone breathing down your neck because you know that you will get the work finished on time, even if it means putting in extra hours to do it.

Size up your boss and decide if it's possible to discuss your differences and find a way to peacefully coexist. If your boss has a history of being inflexible, you may have to resort to other means, such as going over your supervisor's head and discussing the matter with the next level of command. Be careful that this tactic doesn't backfire. Your complaints may fall on deaf ears if this manager has the same type of personality as your boss or generally backs other managers. You're not likely to get anywhere unless you're a highly valued employee.

If there's a chance of making improvements by talking to your boss, use what's called the "assertive approach." This involves discussing problems openly and finding ways to improve the relationship.

Using diplomacy and finesse, state your problem without placing blame for its cause. Direct attention to a solution rather than dwell on the difficulties caused by the problem. Then listen carefully to what the other person has to say to understand why he or she has reacted in a certain manner. You'll learn to negotiate for change more effectively when you understand what this person wants, why it's desirable, and what can be done to make changes—even compromises—so it's a win-win situation for both of you.

Another approach is to work on what career counselor Dr. Richard Citrin calls "reframing your perspective"—looking at your situation from a different point of view to see what can be done to improve matters.

This technique helped Brooke, who worked at a computer company for a new manager who had been promoted because he was a successful salesman, not for his skill in working with subordinates. Brooke disliked her manager's arrogance and his indifference when she asked him questions. She thought he was trying to brush her off.

In counseling sessions, she was encouraged to look at the situation differently to see if she was misinterpreting her boss's actions. We discussed the possibility that her boss wanted her to work more independently, but he didn't know how to tell her that. When Brooke told him that she wanted to consult with him less and work on her own, she discovered that he, too, preferred that she work more independently. Once Brooke did that, she and her boss got along much better.

Sometimes rifts are caused by a simple misunderstanding but require great skill to patch up the relationship. Seeking out knowledgeable people within your organization or an outside mentor can often help you determine the most effective strategy for dealing with your problem.

5. *Redesign your job or transfer to another one*

If you have outgrown your job or found that it wasn't a good match with your talents in the first place, consider other ways to use your skills within the organization. This may involve a lateral move into another department or asking to work on different projects.

You can draw up a general plan for redesigning your job and then present your ideas to your boss. Discuss problems openly and thoroughly with your supervisor, with the attitude of "how can I help to make it better?"

Remember, a perennial complaint from many supervisors is, "If only I had known there was a problem, I could have done something." Your manager may offer suggestions and be willing to clear a pathway for you. Then it's up to you to make it happen.

Consider if there's a place in the company where you'll fit in better. Check job openings posted on bulletin boards or find out through the company grapevine what opportunities are available. R. E. Burgstrum, personnel director of the John Deere Company in Moline, Illinois, complains that "often employees don't try hard enough to change jobs internally." An internal shift may involve a move up, down, or laterally into a different area where you can make better use of your talents.

Just be sure to target jobs that are suitable rather than feel compelled to take what's available. When the chairman of the history department at a California university retired, Dr. Williams, a tenured professor who was extremely well liked by students, was promoted into this position. Dr. Williams felt obligated to take the title because it offered more money and prestige. The problem was, he missed the day-to-day contact with students and didn't particularly like administrative duties. After two years, he was eager to get back into the classroom and asked to resume his earlier duties.

Conversely, other people want to have more influence in their organization. They want to turn cranks, pull levers, not just fine-tune the knobs. To move into a position of more power, seek people who can help you advance and determine what it will take to be noticed. That's the tactic Neale Godfrey used to rise beyond her entry-level position at Chase Manhattan Bank in New York.

Godfrey began a weekly program of inviting department heads to lunch, explaining that she wanted to advance her career by having a better understanding of all banking functions. She learned a lot about the inner workings of the bank through these informal conversations. The valuable contacts she made provided a foundation that helped her rapidly advance and eventually take over, at age thirty-four, as president of First Women's Bank of New York.[1]

Many people are a bit timid about taking the initiative that Godfrey did. They hold back, thinking they will be turned down or won't ever go beyond a certain point. But in many cases, having the courage to be a risk-taker is essential to moving ahead.

Anheuser-Busch's Model Program

Even if your company doesn't offer the extensive career services that Anheuser-Busch provides, their program exemplifies the process that would benefit every employee who's searching for greater job satisfaction.

Anheuser-Busch offers a number of career development programs to help employees find out what opportunities are available in the company and what they should do to prepare themselves to advance. Several times a year the St. Louis, Missouri–based brewer sponsors a two-day seminar on managing personal growth, which helps employees understand themselves better. Staff members look at how they view their position, how their supervisors view them, and what they need to do in their current job to move to the next position. A one-day career development program is also offered to find out what jobs are open, what employees can do to improve themselves, how to write résumés to circulate internally, and how to perform exploratory interviews.

Lincoln Scott, employment services manager at Anheuser-Busch, says, "Each of our recruiters here is available to talk to employees who are interested in making changes. The recruiter will help them set up informational and exploratory interviews, and the recruiter will call the department and tell them someone is interested in a position."

Scott said they urge employees to "talk about the kinds of things the job entails, including the pitfalls. They're encouraged to look at the pluses and minuses of the job." He said employees are also encouraged to ask about job requirements, what kind of skills they need in order to get the job, and if they don't have them, how they can go about acquiring them.

6. *Improve working conditions*

Even if your major dissatisfaction doesn't center around actual working conditions, you may feel better about your job if you enhance your work space, negotiate for a flexible work schedule, or are provided equipment that will help you work more efficiently. Lobby for these improvements by mentioning how this will help you improve your performance.

Let's say you want to cut back on the amount of overtime you must work since your company made staff reductions. You see a more efficient way to streamline the operation by reorganizing assignments and duties.

In order to build support for your ideas, share your thoughts with your co-workers. They could strengthen your cause by backing your proposals at a staff meeting. Later, you could discuss initiating changes with your boss.

Management consultant Dr. Margaret Pinder suggests negotiating for what you want by "expanding the supervisor's list of options." You can say, "I agree this is needed. Would you consider these options?" This approach gets you more involved in the problem-solving process and will likely enable you to get more of what you want.

Some people take the initiative to improve their working conditions on their own. Jodi, a police captain, was transferred to a substation located in a dreary, aging municipal office building. Because the overall look of these quarters lowered morale, Jodi asked for money to renovate. She was told that no more than $200 could be spent, which was too small a sum to hire anyone for the needed work.

That money, however, would cover the cost of paint, so she invited members of her department to attend a Sunday painting party. Many officers volunteered to add the fresh coat of paint, which greatly improved the look of the place.

Drawing up a Plan

Think about what you must do to resolve your job difficulties. Use these suggestions to help you answer the following questions:

1. Set goals that are reachable.
2. Consider realistic ways to achieve your plan.
3. Ask for help and consult additional sources when necessary.
4. Establish realistic deadlines to avoid procrastinating.

Date _____

1. (a) What changes can I make in myself that will improve my job?

   (b) How can I make these changes?

2. (a) What changes can I make in my job that will help me feel more satisfied?

   (b) How can I make these changes?

3. How will things be different when I've achieved these goals?

4. When will I check my progress?

After a few months, you should see some results from the changes you initiated. These improvements will reinforce your decision to stay.

Later on, use the suggestions in this chapter to help rejuvenate your job when you're feeling restless after reaching a plateau, or when you're dealing with another nagging problem. Whether you're dissatisfied or not, it's helpful to periodically do a job assessment to continue growing professionally and enriching your professional life.

If the improvement plan fails to work, reconsider your decision to stay. At least making an effort to salvage your job gives you the satisfaction of knowing you tried. And if it doesn't help, you have a clearer indication that the best solution for you is to find a more rewarding position elsewhere.

9

Should You Find Another Job
Before You Quit or Get Fired?

Leave them while you're looking good.
—Anita Loos

IF you've decided to quit, you have another decision to make before you resign: Do you quit first and then go job-hunting? Or do you attempt to use whatever spare time is available and secure another position before cutting ties?

There are arguments supporting both cases. A lot depends on your field, position, age, employment history, and present value to your company. But as a rule of thumb, we encourage people to practice the wing-walker's motto: "Always have something to grab onto before making your next move." In other words, most people are better off if they line up another job before leaving their present position.

It is a bitter irony, but unemployed job hunters find it more difficult to get jobs than people who have one. Your desirability in the job market is reduced when you're not working. It arouses employers' suspicions, leading them to question: Why are you out of work? Are you capable? Will you be a problem employee?

Barbara Pizzala, human resources associate at W. L. Gore & Associates in Newark, Delaware, voiced a common perception. While acknowledging that there are exceptions, depending on the situation, "With the job market being what it is, the impression I have is that there are jobs out there for people who want to work, who are good at what they do," Pizzala said. "So if you're not working, the implication could be that you're not any good."

During interviews, Pizzala said she finds out why people are unemployed and what they have been doing. If someone has been out of work for a long time—several months to a year—"that's a huge question mark for me," she said.

A person who's out of work may not command as high a starting salary as someone who's being wooed away from another company. Unemployed individuals have less leverage in negotiating for certain job conditions and benefits, especially if they've been out of work for several months. Employers assume someone in this predicament will settle for less just to get a job. It may be worth putting up with a difficult situation long enough to find another position.

Granted, it's not easy to job hunt while employed, but it can pay off in the long run, especially if you can't afford to be out of work for long. As finances dwindle, pressure mounts to find a job. In this situation, people are prone to take any position—suitable or not. And that may set them up for repeating the cycle of being unhappy and wanting to quit.

How to Look for a Job While Still Employed

You may take heart in the fact that an estimated one-third of all job hunters stay employed while searching for a better position.[1] Although looking for work can be very time-consuming, it can be done while on a company's payroll.

Most people must remain discreet about the job search.

If word leaks out, you have to be prepared to clear out your desk sooner than you planned.

In rare cases, you may be able to carry out your quest with the blessings of your employer. If you are absolutely certain your boss will be understanding, announce your plans to leave, but say you would like to continue working until you find another position. If all goes well, you've bought yourself time to job-hunt openly while still receiving a paycheck. In return, you should be committed to maintaining your productivity and facilitating a smooth transition when you turn your work over to someone else.

Here are some common questions about how to job-hunt while still employed:

How do I find time to interview for jobs?

You make time by scheduling meetings before or after work, during lunch hours, weekends, and even holidays. You'd be surprised how many employers would rather see you during off hours to avoid interrupting their busy work day.

Also consider using vacation time for interviews. It often takes that kind of dedication to land a better job.

Be careful not to change your behavior or work routine in a way that will arouse suspicion. One man raised a lot of eyebrows when he started leaving the office two or three times each week for "doctors' appointments." He appeared to be in good health and had taken off few sick days in the past, so people started to assume that something else was going on.

You're likely to make a favorable impression when you tell a job interviewer, "I can't leave my department short-handed. Can we arrange to meet . . ." Then offer several times when you can get away. This statement indicates you are a conscientious worker who thinks about an employer's needs.

111

Do I tell co-workers I'm looking for another job?

In most cases, you should remain mum about your job-hunting activities. Even if you think your closest confidant wouldn't say anything, the word might accidentally slip out and you could be hastily dismissed.

You never know how word may get back to a boss. In one situation, a man was leaving the personnel department of a company where he had just applied for a job when he bumped into a sales representative from his own firm. The salesman snitched on the job hunter, who was fired shortly thereafter.

How do I get the word out that I'm looking for work?

Informal contacts provide leads for almost 75 percent of all successful job searches, according to Harvard sociologist Mark S. Granovetter.[2] To boost your success, pass the word along to people you can trust, including friends, relatives, former co-workers, contacts from professional organizations, acquaintances from school, church, etc. If you write down a list of everyone you know who might have job leads, you'll be surprised at the number of people who might be of help to you.

Use good judgment in deciding who to confide in about your job hunt. Caution your contacts to be discreet if you don't want your present employer to learn about your plans.

How do I uncover leads about unadvertised jobs?

The secret to finding a good position is knowing how to uncover the hidden job market. As many as 80 percent of all jobs are never advertised.[3] Many companies would rather talk to qualified candidates who have been referred by others than be inundated with dozens of people who aren't suitable.

Knowing the importance of tapping into the underground job market, the intrepid job hunter is resourceful and tenacious in checking out many possibilities. The best way to find out about job leads is through networking. A job search is a hunt for information that will lead you to a job opening.

To find out about the unadvertised openings, you can conduct information or exploratory interviews. For example, you may have a friend who can introduce you to a knowledgeable person in the field in which you're interested. The friend of a friend then becomes a source for several job openings or potential openings. People have been known to make such a good impression during these meetings that the contact has even offered them a job.

Look at all available sources, including college career centers, job banks maintained by professional organizations, government job listings in libraries, telephone job information lines with recordings of openings, etc.

Should I contact a headhunter?

If you are thinking of contacting an executive search consultant, or headhunter as they are often called, remember that they're hired by companies to recruit executive-level employees. Most of their time is spent searching for the crème de la crème in a particular profession—usually highly paid, well-respected employed individuals. Then they hope to make them a job offer they can't refuse.

If you happen to be in a high-demand field they specialize in, you may be in luck. If you're not, don't feel bad if headhunters say, "Don't call us, we'll call you."

What results can I expect from want ads?

Want ads appear to be a safe, easy way for employed people to solicit job interviews. They can provide an insight into how many jobs are available in a particular field. And they are useful as long as you remember that the classifieds only help about 10 percent of the population locate jobs.[4] Knowing this, you don't want to spend a majority of your time answering classified ads when you have a better chance of finding a job through networking.

Consider the company that advertises in *The Wall Street Journal.* As many as six hundred people may respond. Out of these, the personnel director asks a secretary to separate the applicants into two stacks according to salary requirements, prior experience, and age. The company happens to be looking for someone under thirty who has at least three years' experience in a specific area, and will accept a salary of $25,000 a year or less.

When the secretary is finished, only ten applicants qualify. That means 590 people aren't even considered.

With these odds in mind, you can see how slim your chances are of even being interviewed for advertised jobs. Go ahead and reply to want ads, because they do work. Just be sure to use other job-hunting techniques as well.

Be especially careful when answering "blind" ads, those which don't list company names. You may inadvertently send a résumé to your own company. People have been fired for such blunders.

How helpful are employment agencies?

The value of employment agencies depends on the quality of the firm, the type of work you desire, your experience, and the number of contacts you have. Don't expect an agency to do the work for you or have a lead on every suitable job.

Find an agency that specializes in your field. Be sure you check all resources before accepting a job that requires you to pay a fee to the agency. Register first with state-run employment agencies and personnel firms whose fees are paid by the employer before you try a place where you will have to hand over a percentage of your hard-earned salary.

What should I include in a job résumé?

Revise your résumé to highlight your accomplishments. By merely listing dates of employment and job titles, the employer has no idea of what you've done in the past, what makes you special. Stating specific achievements using active verbs will create a much better impression. For example, listing that you "increased profits by 10 percent through initiating cost-cutting measures" is certainly an attention-grabber. Generally, a résumé should be no more than two pages, and formatted so that it can be easily scanned by an interviewer.

As with everything, there are exceptions. Employers have different preferences about résumé length and content. It often depends on the field, type of company, and individual likes and dislikes. For example, James Ketcham, director of professional recruitment at Kollmorgen Corporation in Stamford, Connecticut, said that he's a technically oriented person and likes detailed chronological résumés. He hires many engineers, and he likes to know what size company the person has worked for in the past, previous salary, and why they left—even if they were fired. "It doesn't bother me at all when I get a résumé from someone who's been fired," Ketcham added. He tries to find out why someone was fired before he decides if it's a concern.

How can I make a good impression in a job interview?

Because most people are hired on the basis of the "chemistry" between them and the employer during an interview, preparation is vital. Job interviews are often brief and you'll

What Type of Résumés Catch an Employer's Eye?

Think of your résumé as a sales piece or a calling card that in two short pages sums up why you are an ideal employee. Here are ways in which your résumé will stand out from the one hundred or more that may cross the employer's desk each week.

• At first glance, your résumé is easy to read, perfectly typeset with no typos or misspellings.
• The résumé and cover letter reflect your careful targeting of this company and indicate that you have the right qualifications. You don't appear to be doing a mass mailing to every company in your field. You have even revised your résumé to highlight the skills this company desires.
• Your résumé concisely sums up what makes you special. You have listed specific accomplishments and mentioned enough about your work history and education that the employer can accurately predict whether you will fit in or not.

need to make points in a very short time.

Many people find job interviews nerve-racking, but the better prepared you are, the more confident you'll feel. There are many standard questions asked in all interviews. Think about how you would respond to the following:

• Tell me about yourself. (Your response should be kept brief and upbeat, with the focus on key career achievements.)
• Why do you want to change jobs?
• What kind of job are you looking for now?

- What are your long-range objectives?
- What are your salary requirements?
- When could you be available to start here?
- Tell me about your present company.
- What kind of [employee/manager] are you?
- How would you describe yourself?
- What are your strengths and weaknesses? (We've found that people tend to be a little *too* forthcoming about their weaknesses. Perhaps it's a desire to appear honest, but remember, you're competing with other applicants and need to accentuate the positive.)
- Describe your present boss.
- Who can I talk to about your performance?
- Are you open to relocation?
- How long have you been looking for a new job?
- Why are you interested in this company? (This is an opportunity to show you've done your homework and have specific assets you can bring to the organization.)[5]

After you've formed responses to these requests and questions, stage a mock job interview with a friend or family member assuming the role of the employer. If that's not possible, practice alone. In either situation, tape-record the session. Listen to the way you phrase answers. Do you respond in a confident and direct fashion? Do you have good solid examples to back up your claims about particular skills you possess? Keep working at your responses until you've created a concise and upbeat answer to every important question your interviewer may ask. (In chapter 10, you'll learn how to handle questions about sensitive issues, such as getting fired or quitting under less than ideal circumstances.)

Be sure to bring a list of at least three people who will give you a good recommendation. If you have any doubts about what they might say, phone them and ask how they'd respond if a potential employer called for a reference. If an interviewer asks about calling a previous supervisor who will say something negative, tell the interviewer in advance what you expect will be said. Then offer an explanation of why you won't receive a favorable report. It will help to hear your side of the story first.

Your interviewing skills can improve with each encounter. You'll probably feel good about the way you handled some questions and may realize that you can improve your delivery in other areas. After the interview, ask yourself these questions:

1. Overall, did I handle the interview effectively? Why or why not?
2. Was I invited for a second interview? Why or why not?
3. Did I explain any previous job problems in a way that let the interviewer know what I learned from the experience?
4. Did I discuss how my skills and achievements in the past can help me contribute to this company?
5. Did I talk too much or too little?
6. Was I appropriately dressed, based on the attire of others at the company?
7. Was I honest in providing information that will jibe with what previous employers and references will say?
8. Did I say anything negative about former bosses, colleagues, or organizations?
9. What can I do to be more effective in the next interview?

Sometimes Quitting First Is a Viable Option

Even considering the drawbacks, you may decide quitting is more desirable. If you're in a field with lots of employment opportunities, you won't run the risk of being out of work long.

There are many different circumstances that warrant quitting first. You may travel so much you have no time to job hunt. Or your company may offer such an attractive early retirement package it's too good to turn down.

Also, some of you in certain fields or high-level positions may feel it's necessary to take a break to recharge and reevaluate your needs before moving on to something else. And of course, some work situations are so untenable that sticking around until you have another job offer is simply unbearable.

When the ax is about to fall

It's also prudent to move on when you think you may be fired. If you quit, you probably won't be eligible for unemployment benefits as quickly as you would be if you were fired, but that may be a small price to pay.

It's true that today getting fired isn't the bane of one's career that it once was. However, being terminated is a demoralizing experience, even if you don't have much respect for your employer. Also, when you interview for another job, it's much easier to explain quitting than getting fired.

Unfortunately, not everyone recognizes the warning signs of imminent termination. Even when people do, they sometimes choose to remain where they are because they can't face the prospect of looking for another job.

Kyle refused to read the signals that he was in danger of losing his job as personnel director of a telecommunications company. When he was hired he had been told the firm was a people-oriented organization, and yet he failed to acknowledge the fact that, in practice, the chief executive officer was bottom-line oriented. Rather than accept that companies sometimes perform in ways that are inconsistent with their stated philosophies, Kyle persistently attempted to implement people-oriented programs, ultimately incurring the wrath of the C.E.O. If he had "read the environment," he could have made the decision to modify his behavior or resign before he was asked to leave.

If you get the feeling that somebody's itching to hand you a pink slip, it's time to take action. Here are some warning signs.

- Relationships between you and people who count have deteriorated over a period of time.
- You were transferred to a position of less importance or "put on the shelf," where you have little impact on the operation.
- You aren't invited to major decision-making meetings.
- You no longer have as much authority, supervise as many people, or have as many important responsibilities.
- Your boss seems to give you the cold shoulder and won't take time to discuss matters.
- You are moved to a smaller, less-desirable office.
- You are asked to share a secretary with someone else.
- Perks that you enjoyed, such as a company car, are taken away from you.
- You complete an assignment and it's shelved.
- You have been warned that people are unhappy with your overall performance.
- Cutbacks appear imminent and your job is one of the most dispensable.

If you suspect you are in trouble, arrange a meeting to clear the air to discuss whether your supervisor is unhappy with your work. Many bosses find it difficult to confront employees and give them face-to-face evaluations. If you discover during your conversation that your supervisor is indeed unhappy with you and the situation seems unsalvageable, then it's time to plan your departure.

Depending on how you read the situation, you may want to give two weeks' notice shortly after that meeting. During this time, prepare yourself for the transition to unemployment. Utilize your benefits package while you still have it and schedule any medical or dental appointments you've been putting off. And you may want to take care of other matters such as extending your line of credit or getting a loan to tide you over in case you run out of money before you find another job.

The important thing is that you confront your situation and then choose the best course of action before your boss chooses one for you.

10

What to Say in Job Interviews

about Quitting or Getting Fired

When in doubt, tell the truth.

—Mark Twain

BEING prepared to answer probing questions in a job interview can make the difference between landing a coveted position or receiving a polite rejection letter. A question asked by practically every interviewer is: "Why do you want to leave your job?" Employers will be especially interested in your most recent position, and some may go back as far as your very first job.

By asking about transitions in your work life, an employer is searching for clues about the type of employee you will be. How you've behaved in the past is an indication of what you'll do in the future. The interviewer will be looking for both positive and negative signs. By knowing what types of statements will typically alarm an interviewer, you can avoid making some casual comment that will send up a red flag. But just as important as avoiding negatives, you'll know how to present your good points in a way that will push the interviewer's "hire" button.

Walt Disney Studios' Kurtis Kishi said personnel managers in general often look for motivational factors to determine why a person made certain choices in his or her career path. "What you're trying to do is get into the essence of what really motivates this person to make job choices and see how that correlates with what we have to offer here, both at present and maybe down the road."

Handling Sensitive Issues

How do you address the times in your work life that you'd just as soon sweep under the rug and forget, although there's no way to hide them? How do you discuss previous problems with a prospective employer without jeopardizing your chances of getting hired? It may be tempting to have a pat answer or bend the truth to create a good impression. But phoniness can be detected by astute interviewers. You have far more to gain by answering questions with a truthful, carefully phrased response. Interviewers may check with previous employers to see if your story jibes with what they say.

Here are some tips on discussing job problems:

1. Determine in advance how you'll summarize your experience in a candid and concise manner.
2. Explain what you learned from the experience.
3. Avoid blaming previous employers for job problems. If you're judgmental, the interviewer will wonder who was *really* at fault.
4. Turn the focus away from the problem and stress your strengths, goals, and what you can contribute to the prospective employer.

A good way to blow an interview is to unload complaints about a former boss or office politics that unfairly drove you out the door. Using the interview to vent your frustrations about present or past jobs may leave the impression that you are a chronic complainer.

Giving an incomplete explanation of why you quit is also damaging. If you say too little, the interviewer may think the worst.

Many thorough interviews include a number of potentially tricky questions such as the following:

Have you ever been fired?

Being fired has become commonplace in the private sector, and does not have the stigma it once did. Many people end up improving their situation in the same manner as Lee Iacocca, who was fired by the Ford Motor Company and then went on to rebuild the Chrysler Corporation.

Karla Leavelle, assistant vice-president of employee relations at a Dallas bank, says she doesn't have any preconceived notions when an applicant mentions being terminated. "I consider the industry. It may be one undergoing a lot of change and the person could have gotten fired after a merger or acquisition. I ask the reason why a person was fired and then check references to verify."

Individuals who have been fired are often bitter about the experience. During the interview, avoid dwelling on the fact that you may have been treated unfairly. Briefly relate the circumstances, and if possible, note that you have had better experiences elsewhere, before or since the termination.

Here's how Sandra discussed her situation: "I was working as the program director at a radio station when the ratings slipped several points. Not long afterward, I was fired. It really caught me by surprise because I thought I'd done the best I could. In any event, what I learned at that job helped me improve the music format at the next station where I worked. We advanced from the number five to the number two station in the market."

This explanation indicates that Sandra's firing was linked to rating points—a common occurrence in the broadcast industry. When Sandra said the firing was unexpected, the interviewer realized Sandra wasn't given time to improve her work performance.

Sandra wisely discussed how she used what she learned to improve the music format at the next station. And she used a specific example—an increase in rating points—to illustrate personal achievement. Whenever possible, discuss actual accomplishments so that an employer clearly understands your capabilities.

What do you dislike about your present job and/or boss?
Interviewers will ask leading questions such as this one to uncover your true feelings. If you dodge the question, they'll wonder why. If you launch into a long discourse about your unbearable job or knock your present employer, the interviewer may think you're overly critical.

It's best to keep your complaints short and to the point. Making a general statement about a job problem is the recommended way to state your case without sounding like a chronic complainer. For example, if you're making a switch because your advancement opportunities have been limited, you can simply say this without adding that you're angry at being passed over for a promotion.

This advice also applies to comments about your boss. The interviewer is less likely to be alarmed if you say, "The president of the company and I have different management styles" rather than, "I can't stand working for that jerk."

John Komer, interviewing and placement specialist at Southwest Airlines in Dallas, said, "If someone says they have had trouble with management, it may raise a yellow flag, not a red flag until I find out the circumstances. If they feel like they have been singled out—a me-versus-them situation—then I'm concerned." He seeks people who will fit in with Southwest Airlines' corporate culture and will have the philosophy of looking at what they can do for the company instead of being overly concerned with what the company can do for them.

Here's how Brandon diplomatically responded to why he left an unhappy situation: "My supervisor and I differ over the direction of our department. I respect his opinion but need to work for a progressive company that shares some of the ideas I have for building sales. My boss doesn't have any hard feelings about my resignation. In fact, when you check with him he'll tell you about the contributions I've made, including . . ."

This response takes a potentially damaging situation and focuses on the applicant's need to work for a company that has similar goals to his. The employee avoids making the boss sound like the "bad guy," even though he was very difficult to work for. Brandon concludes on a positive note by mentioning that the supervisor will give him a good recommendation. He then goes on to list specific accomplishments.

Why do you want to leave your current job or why did you leave previous jobs?

The interviewer asks such a question to determine if you're leaving (or have left) under favorable circumstances. Your response also indicates how well you performed on the job and whether you will treat other employers fairly.

The most common positive reply to this question is: "I'm looking for better job opportunities." This response reflects no animosity. If it's your real reason, state it.

There are numerous other reasons for leaving a job. As we noted in chapter 2, some are considered justifiable and others raise eyebrows. Below are several reasons for quitting that will make an interviewer wary. In each sample, an employee offers two different statements of the truth —one version is potentially damaging, the other more positive and reassuring to the interviewer.

Personality conflicts

JOHN (detrimental response): "I quit working for a large architectural firm because my boss and I didn't get along."

Why it's detrimental: When an interviewee mentions personality conflicts, employers will wonder who has the most disagreeable personality—the applicant or the former employer. Be careful about discussing interpersonal conflicts. Interviewers will be concerned that you have a problem with authority or have difficulty getting along with people.

JOHN (positive response): "My boss and I had different approaches to projects. I want to work for someone who allows me to work as part of a team and share my ideas. He preferred to call all the shots and then closely supervised everyone to make sure his orders were carried out. The management style of a previous employer allowed me to be more creative, and as a result, I made significant contributions that enhanced the efficiency of our operation."

Why it's positive: This answer takes the focus away from the conflict and avoids criticism of the boss. John discusses how he does well when he's given an opportunity to be more creative. He doesn't run on at length about a stifling situation. By mentioning good experiences at other jobs, John indicates that he has gotten along well with other types of people.

Work was too demanding

PEG (detrimental response): "I quit the insurance company because of excessive overtime. The company demanded too much of me and everyone else."

Why it's detrimental: The interviewer may wonder why so much overtime was required. Did Peg contribute to the need for overtime in any way by being disorganized? Will she balk at occasionally working extra hours in a new position? This matter may be of special concern to today's employers who operate "lean and mean" with only the minimal number of personnel. They'll be wary of someone who they think may not carry his or her fair share of the work load.

PEG (positive response): "Because our company is under-staffed, it's customary for most people in the claims department to put in overtime—a fifty- to sixty-hour week is typical. I attempt to use my time wisely and work as efficiently as possible. However, I still work so many extra hours that I've been neglecting my family. I realize many jobs require overtime now and then and I don't mind that. My objection is working fifty-plus hours a week on a regular basis."

Why it's positive: Peg makes it clear that her complaint is with *excessive* overtime, not with working overtime occasionally when needed. She also quells any fears the employer might have about whether she managed her time well.

Personal problems

AMY (detrimental response): "I resigned as the night nursing supervisor because I was going through a divorce."

Why it's detrimental: Employers will be concerned about whether Amy's personal matters have been resolved or will continue to affect her work performance. In addition, they may question whether Amy has the emotional stability and maturity to handle another personal crisis. Many administrators have sympathy for employees who are experiencing difficulties such as a divorce, loss of a loved one, or major illnesses. But they need reassurance that the person will be strong enough to deal with the difficulties and not let work slide for too long.

AMY (positive response): "I quit to get my life back in order during a divorce. Rather than let my work suffer, I decided to leave and take care of personal business and legal matters. I moved back to my hometown, where my parents can help me with child care. The divorce is final and I'm eager to begin work again."

Why it's positive: This answer focuses on business and legal arrangements rather than emotional upsets. Amy explains what happened and indicates that the difficult times are over now that the divorce is final. Mentioning that arrangements have been made for child care is a sign that Amy is ready to work again.

Pursuit of rapid advancement

BLAINE (detrimental response): "I've worked for three different airlines in five years because I'm determined to be a midlevel manager by the time I'm thirty-five. When I've been held back from advancing, I've sought other opportunities."

Why it's detrimental: This answer reflects selfish motives and leaves the impression Blaine has little consideration for employers. By saying the job held him back, Blaine fails to take responsibility for what happened.

BLAINE (positive response): "I know three jobs in five years may sound like a lot, but I'd like to explain what happened. A year after I started the first job, the airline merged with another. My job was phased out and I declined the offer to retrain for another position. I thought I could advance at another regional carrier but realized after a year that a promotion was unlikely because the supervisors in my department were there to stay. I went to work for a larger airline and was promoted to a first-line supervisor after six months. Now this airline has a hiring freeze and is cutting back on international routes. My prospects for advancement have dimmed considerably. That's why I want to work with a more dynamic airline. I've studied the industry and believe I can find long-term satisfaction here."

Why it's positive: The explanation offers more insight into Blaine's motives. The first company merged; the second was too small; and the third fell victim to a downturn in the industry. Blaine isn't blaming anyone or saying he's unwilling to stay with one company. The final statement indicates that Blaine seeks long-term employment under more favorable circumstances.

Burnout

HARRY (detrimental response): "I quit my job as a social worker because I couldn't cope with the stress."

Why it's detrimental: If Harry can't deal with pressures at one job, an interviewer will wonder how well he will cope somewhere else. Most jobs involve a certain amount of stress. Employers will wonder if Harry has other problems that make it difficult for him to keep up with demands.

HARRY (positive response): "As you know, many social workers handle an excessive number of cases. I coped with the pressure for three years until our department didn't have the funds to replace people who quit. Finally, I became so frustrated by not being able to give much attention to even the most serious cases that I took a short leave of absence to consider whether I wanted to stay in the field.

During that time, I decided to make a switch to a private charity organization."

Why it's positive: This statement reiterates common problems experienced by social workers. Harry mentions he had handled difficult situations for several years until deciding it was in his best interest to move to another type of job. He also mentions that he had taken time out to carefully contemplate this move.

If you have a questionable reason for leaving your current job or previous position, think about how you can fully explain what happened. The objective is to discuss the situation in such a way that the employer won't be concerned the problem will crop up again. Stress what you can contribute to the organization. By emphasizing what you can do to benefit the company, you're likely to make a favorable impression.

11

How to Evaluate a Job Offer

It's odd—but telling—that American companies are rarely examined from the standpoint of their employees.

—Robert Levering, Milton Moskowitz,
and Michael Katz, *The 100 Best Companies
to Work for in America*

ONCE you get a job offer, you're faced with another decision: Is it really in your best interest to accept? Will you fit in at the new company? What if you find out later you made a big mistake?

All too often, people fail to carefully evaluate a job opportunity, then regret it later. There's a tendency to take the first firm offer that comes along in order to flee from a bad situation. They may get swept up in the excitement of receiving a job offer. Marsha, for instance, allowed herself to be seduced by the prospect of becoming a manager in a young, rapidly expanding company. As a result, she ignored rumors that her prospective boss was uncomfortable sharing responsibility. After all, she later recalled, during the interview her boss had assured her that delegation wouldn't be a problem. Once on the job Marsha learned that the rumors were true, and her dream job quickly became a nightmare.

Interviewers Paint a Rosy Picture

Take an objective look at the job and consider both the negative and positive aspects. There's a tendency to hear only positive aspects of a position from the person who's trying to win you over. At the same time, interviewers tend to gloss over job descriptions. This is particularly true if the company is new, the position has just been created, or the job is difficult to fill.

Misunderstandings also occur when a person is interviewed by several people in the company, including someone in the personnel department who may not have a clear understanding of the job duties. The interviewer may give a sketchy description of the basic responsibilities. Sometimes the job simply isn't well defined, which is often the case in smaller companies, where people may perform several functions. And in some instances, companies just plain lie to attract a particular person or to fill an unappealing job.

The Reality Check

To make sure you won't be misled, here are some basic considerations to keep in mind while you assess your prospective job:

Is this really a firm offer?

As elementary as it might sound, make sure you have a definite job offer. Misunderstandings can occur when people think they'll be offered a position and then find out there's been an eleventh-hour change. Will the person you talk to make the final decision or must several people reach joint agreement? Be sure *everyone* wants you. You could find out the company president has overruled everyone else and is bringing in his or her favorite candidate.

You don't want to end up like Frank, a salesman who planned to switch from his financially troubled company to a more stable business. He talked to a woman in a middle-management position who said her company was very interested in creating a job for him.

He was so anxious to bail out of his floundering company that he hastily resigned and then telephoned the woman to say he was ready to start work. When he reached her, she sounded rather flustered and said they couldn't afford to hire him just now but might be able to in a few months. Suddenly Frank found himself not only without a job, but without a firm job prospect.

Will I be satisfied with this position?

While you think about what you really want from a job, consider how closely this position meets your needs. As you evaluate what you don't like, consider whether you will be able to change conditions or learn to live with them.

Many people are reluctant to ask probing questions in an interview. But you shouldn't be. An interview is an opportunity to learn details about the job opening. You should feel free to ask as many questions as the interviewer asks you. Don't hesitate to bring up such matters as:

- What are the job's responsibilities?
- To whom will I report, and what is his or her background?
- Why is the job available?
- What are the opportunities for advancement?
- Does the job involve travel?
- What is the salary range?
- What benefits are provided?
- What is the company's relocation policy?

- When will an offer be made?
- When would I have to start?

The more questions you ask about the job, the more you'll get a sense of not only its positive aspects, but the drawbacks as well.

Be sure to double-check what you hear from secondhand sources, such as a headhunter. Less reputable individuals have been known to misrepresent jobs in hopes of earning a tidy commission.

Will I be satisfied with the company?

Take an objective look at the company. Consider all aspects of the operation, such as the people, corporate culture, and the management style, to determine if you'd feel comfortable in this environment. Be observant about everything you see and hear while meeting with company representatives.

Ask for a tour of the company. Look for small clues that illuminate what it would be like to work for the firm, such as the way receptionists and secretaries deal with other employees and customers. The support staff's attitude, degree of professionalism, and method of handling people often reflects whether a company is properly managed.

The best source for what life is really like in the company is a present or former employee. Even if you don't have a contact to relay inside information, talk to people in the field about the company's reputation. Often suppliers are good sources because they know whether the business pays its bills and treats people right. Look at the firm's brochures, policy manuals, and orientation videos if possible. Find out what the company's written policy is regarding treatment of employees, customers, suppliers, and competitors. See how well its objectives match your own.

Also note whether the firm is employee-oriented. The

following list describes attributes and benefits common to corporations where employee satisfaction is high. You can't expect to find all of the qualities listed below at any one company, but you should expect to find a number of them.

- Employees feel that they are members of a corporate "family" and everyone pulls together as part of the team.
- There is pride in offering quality products or services.
- Pay is competitive and benefit packages go beyond basic medical insurance, often including a profit-sharing or pension plan.
- Employees are kept informed of important matters, even negative issues.
- The physical environment is appealing and conducive to working efficiently.
- The company is sufficiently staffed to avoid excessive overtime.
- The company avoids layoffs if possible.
- People are promoted from within whenever possible.
- Professional growth is encouraged through tuition reimbursement, training programs, seminars, etc.
- Good health is encouraged through wellness programs and concern for overall well-being.
- Concern is shown for an employee's family through child-care assistance, time off to compensate for travel or overtime, etc.

Final Discussions about the Job Offer

The final round of talks should clear up any questions you may have. Firm up all details about the job offer. Some organizations provide a standard contract that spells out exactly what's promised.

Special terms you desire should be negotiated during this session. For example, you may be able to receive a higher salary than was originally offered. Companies usually have a range of pay for the position and you may qualify for the maximum amount, provided you can persuade your employer that your experience and/or talents justify the top salary.

Fringe benefits may also be negotiable, such as a company car, health club membership, paid parking, or other perks. If you want special concessions, such as extra vacation days, request them at this time. Consider not only what you want today, but what you may want in the future, which might include reimbursement for special college courses or training. Employers are often more willing to negotiate during the "courtship" period in order to enhance the attractiveness of the job. Once you're on board, it may be a different story.

Employers may even change job responsibilities or alter a title to fit a person's experience and abilities. You may be surprised at how far employers will go to hire someone they want.

For example, Lindsay assumed she wouldn't be considered for an office manager's position because the company needed someone to start a month before she could get away from her current job. Also, she was tempted to turn down the offer because she didn't think she could get time off to take a three-week European vacation she had paid for in advance.

When she discussed these matters, company officials offered to make special concessions in her case because they were eager to hire her. She was allowed to start work a month later and was given three weeks off without pay to enjoy her trip.

Turning Down the Job Offer

If you see too many drawbacks to the job, prepare to decline the offer. As soon as you're sure—and you should make up your mind within a week—call the person who offered you the position and announce your decision. It is usually unnecessary to go into a long discussion about why you don't want to work there.

The best policy is to simply say, "I appreciate your offer, but I've decided to stay where I am." Make additional comments if you want to be considered for other positions in the future. You could say, "The job we talked about doesn't appear to be right for me, but I would like to be considered for other openings."

Properly handling this discussion is important because you want to avoid any bad feelings. You never know when or where you'll deal with the same people again.

The employer may still try to win you over by sweetening the job offer and making the position more attractive. This could make a big difference and tempt you to reconsider. Ask for additional time to think it over if you're unsure. Be absolutely certain that you'll quit your present position before formally accepting the job offer. Otherwise, you may find yourself in the embarrassing position of agreeing to take a new job and then changing your mind.

Accepting the Job Offer

If you're convinced you should take the job, you must decide who to tell first—your present employer or the people who offered you the job. The protocol in this matter will depend on many factors, including whether you expect any problems or counteroffers. If you suspect the new company may waver on any promises, let your prospective employer know you are ready to accept the position. Go over what you've been promised and include special conditions in a contract or letter of agreement if these documents are common in your industry.

If you think your boss will try to convince you to stay, consider having a meeting to say that you've received a job offer. These discussions can be tricky because the boss may give you his or her blessing and wish you well, or offer to go to great lengths to keep you. In one very unusual situation, a manager even joined a rally staged by staff members who didn't want a popular department head to go to work for a competitor—he'd already given his two weeks' notice. The department head had felt unappreciated and ill-used, but he was so touched by the display of placards and chanting outside his office window, along with the hefty salary increase he was offered, that he decided to stay.

Other people won't have to wrangle with these types of decisions. They may decide to take the job offer and then begin preparing for the formal resignation. Ultimately, your goal is to accept or decline the job offer in the most professional manner possible.

12

How to Handle the Resignation

*If at first you don't succeed, try, try again; then quit—
there's no use being a damn fool about it.*

—W. C. Fields

THERE are two ways to quit: you can make a graceful exit or leave thumbing your nose. If you think you've been poorly treated by your employer or colleagues, you may be tempted to get back at them with a parting shot. After all, you think, what can they do to me now?

Unfortunately, some employees' most creative moments have been their acrimonious parting gestures. One guy we know vented his frustrations with his insensitive, power-hungry boss by transmitting his resignation letter to every computer terminal at his firm. In it, his criticism of his five-foot-three-inch boss opened with the comment, "Mr. —— is not only a small man in stature . . ."

Another acquaintance of ours wanted to get back at a disagreeable co-worker. The departing employee called his colleague at home—on his day off—and in a credible imitation of his boss's distinctive Southern drawl, told the guy he was fired for failing to show up for work. The perpetrator was long gone by the time the distraught co-worker rushed into the office to get his job back.

Vengeful farewells may be deliciously satisfying at the

141

time, but they may come back to haunt you. In many industries, word travels fast when an employee sticks it to an employer. Not knowing all the facts, some prospective employers may assume the worker is simply a troublemaker who will cause them the same kind of grief.

Also, taking revenge may hurt the wrong people. For instance, a woman quit during her firm's busiest season to "shake up management" and make them realize her department was understaffed. The timing of her resignation forced her colleagues, whom she liked, to take on more of the work load. The co-workers resented how this woman's departure accomplished little other than to burden them with more projects.

A Proper Farewell

On the other hand, we know of individuals who have left jobs on such friendly terms that they were later offered a better post at the same company. Hal, a middle-management executive at a New York corporation, resigned to take a job in Los Angeles. His supervisors were sorry to see him go but realized he could advance faster someplace else. They told him to keep in touch. He did, and fourteen months later they called to offer him a newly created position that was two levels higher than the job he left. He moved back to take the job.

Another benefit of leaving on friendly terms is that you never know when you might cross paths with former colleagues or supervisors. A marketing executive learned this when his former boss was hired as his company's new vice-president of sales. Fortunately, the marketing executive had left his previous job on good terms and could look forward to working amicably with his old boss.

There are many ways you can gain from making a graceful departure from your company. Resigning is usually stressful enough without compounding the situation by staging a dramatic showdown. You'll stand a much better chance of getting good job recommendations if you leave with relationships intact. Sometimes there are unexpected benefits. One employee we know was given extra pay for a week of vacation that she hadn't earned—her boss was simply grateful for her conscientiousness. Others have been able to keep their office and secretarial support while they looked for another job.

Planning Your Departure

Before you barge into your boss's office and blurt "I quit," think how you can set the stage for the announcement. Carefully planning what to say will help guarantee a better reception to your announcement.

Also, think about what you may want to negotiate, such as how much time you'll spend finishing projects before you leave. Balance your needs with those of the company. If possible, avoid dumping unfinished projects in someone else's lap. But also be fair to yourself—don't agree to remain so long that you'll fail to give yourself time to prepare for your new job or even take a much-deserved vacation.

Here are some basic considerations that will help you get through the process:

How much notice should I give?

Most companies expect two weeks, although it varies according to a person's position and the employer's requirements. A college president, for example, may need to give up to a year's notice; engineers in a defense firm may be asked to leave the day they resign. In a questionnaire we sent to personnel directors employed by companies selected for *The 100 Best Companies to Work for in America,* 80 percent said that two weeks is their standard requirement,

8 percent said three to four weeks is better, and 12 percent had other requirements.

"It varies by level of position," said Vicki Milledge of Apple Computer, Incorporated, in Cupertino, California. "We 'walk out' some people the day they resign for security or morale reasons. This rarely happens, however."

At other companies, it's common for "problem employees" or people who work in sensitive areas to leave the day they give notice. Anheuser-Busch prefers two weeks' notice in writing, but company officials have the option of letting a person leave that day and giving them two weeks' pay.

At John Deere, it depends on the job. "In highly sensitive positions, the employee would not be permitted to continue to work but would be paid up to one month of salary," R. E. Burgstrum said.

If inadequate notice is given at Kollmorgen Corporation, this fact will be noted during reference checks. "We think it's bad when a person does that," said James Ketcham, director of professional recruitment. "Matter of fact, I had a woman working for me who gave me four days' notice after working here for four years. I didn't like it."

Give your firm adequate time to start looking for your successor and preparing for your departure, but don't spend too much time as a lame-duck employee. Plan on staying just long enough to finish projects and tie up loose ends before your final day.

What's the protocol for announcing a resignation?

The standard procedure is to announce your plans to your immediate supervisor and hand in your letter of resignation during this meeting. It may be tempting to confide in your buddies at work and tell them you're quitting, but think what would happen if your boss learned of your departure from one of them first.

In the survey of personnel directors from *The 100 Best*

Companies, 67 percent said a talk with the boss and a letter of resignation are recommended. The remainder believe a talk with the supervisor is sufficient.

You may want to inform other higher-ups, too, by meeting with them or sending them a letter. It gives you a chance to pass along a personal word of thanks and explain why you're leaving. If you think your boss may provide a slightly distorted version of your departure, by all means, talk to them, too.

When should I announce my plans?

Friday is often a good day to resign because you have the weekend to recover—or celebrate. Choose a day when your supervisor is least likely to be distracted or upset by your announcement. You may find it advantageous to make an announcement that coincides with the end of a pay period or completion of a major project.

Remember that timing can be critical. Few bosses like to be caught off guard, which is what happened to one woman whose subordinate announced his resignation during the office Christmas party. The day after this embarrassing incident, the supervisor called the man into her office and told him he needn't stick around for two weeks. She wanted him out as soon as possible.

Relay your news under optimum conditions. The best bet is to arrange a specific time to meet with your boss by saying something to the effect of, "I need to talk with you privately about an important matter. It'll take about fifteen minutes. When would be a good time today?"

Writing your resignation letter will help you decide what to say when you announce your decision in person.

What should be stated in a resignation letter?

Keep in mind that the resignation letter will be around years after you're gone. Many go into an employee's permanent file. The letter may be checked in the future when an employer wants to know about your work history. If it sounds bitter and critical, it may result in a less than enthusiastic recommendation.

A case in point is an electronics worker who wrote an eleven-page diatribe about the problems with his company and how he would improve them. No one seriously considered his suggestions, and he ended up offending quite a few people in the process.

The best bet is to write a brief, simple letter with neutral comments. Here are the major points to cover:

- A simple statement that you are resigning
- When your resignation will be effective
- Plans for making a smooth transition
- Thanks for your supervisor's help (optional)
- A positive note to conclude the letter

The following pages show samples of two resignation letters. The first is an example of an appropriate letter.

This letter is simple and to the point. The first paragraph contains a brief statement about how long Elizabeth will stay before leaving. Overall, the letter reinforces what will be said during the meeting when she announces her resignation. It avoids unnecessary criticism and makes a positive statement about working at the company. The comment about preparing her files for her successor suggests Elizabeth has considered how she can help make the transition easier for the company.

You aren't expected to state specific reasons why you are leaving or what you will do after you quit. Elizabeth states that she's pursuing "other job opportunities." That statement is preferable to a negative comment, such as complaining about not getting a promotion.

May 1, 1990

Mr. Jack Sorenson
Excel, Inc.
2100 Baxter Ave.
Burbank, Calif. 91505

Dear Mr. Sorenson,

After careful consideration, I've decided to leave the company. My last day will be May 23. Making the decision to resign has been difficult because I've enjoyed the past three years. You were especially helpful when I started and I've appreciated your continued guidance.

I am leaving to pursue other job opportunities. During the next two weeks, I'll finish my final project and get my files in order for my successor. If you have any questions after I'm gone, feel free to call me.

Thanks again for your help and support. I hope we can stay in touch.

Sincerely,

Elizabeth Berger

The next letter is an example of what a disgruntled employee might write.

May 1, 1990

Gordon Ware
Raider Corp.
1593 Dexter St.
Lincoln, Nebr. 91505

Dear Mr. Ware,

I am resigning my position because I'm fed up with the low pay and lack of advancement opportunities. As you know, I haven't been happy for a long time. Nothing has been done to resolve the situation, so I have no choice but to quit.

I want you to know that part of my dissatisfaction stems from the fact that you fail to delegate work properly. I felt like I had to carry more than my share of the work in this department.

I've sent a copy of this letter to your supervisor.

Sincerely,

Roger Martin

The bitter tone of this letter may encourage Roger's supervisor to tell him to leave immediately. It's doubtful his criticism will be taken seriously when it is expressed in this manner.

You can also go to the other extreme, as the employee who turned in a two-word resignation letter: "I quit!" When his supervisor read the "letter," it had the same effect on him as an obscene gesture. The message the employee conveyed was: "I don't have enough respect for you boneheads to bother writing a formal resignation later." In this case, saying too little was just as harmful as saying too much.

Be sure to carefully word your letter if you're leaving under less-than-ideal circumstances. Stick to basic comments about your plans to leave, how much notice you are giving, and what you will do before your last day.

What should be said when resigning?

If you find resigning difficult—and most people will—plan in advance how you will say "I quit." Granted, it may sound like a canned speech, but thinking ahead about your talk will help you avoid saying something you'll regret later. Here are the major points to include in your talk:

- *When you plan to leave.* Give a firm date. If you have time, you might offer to stick around longer than two weeks to train a successor or to finish up other projects.
- *What work you plan to complete.* A simple status report of what will be done and left undone will help the boss reassign projects.
- *Why you want to quit.* A brief statement will suffice. Although you're not really obligated to spell out why you're leaving, your boss will probably ask if you don't explain. Be careful how you phrase your response. It's best to stick with the positive benefits of the job you've accepted, and avoid the negative comments about the situation you're leaving.
- *Where you plan to go.* This is optional. Disclosing where you're headed is your choice. But you may be asked if you don't volunteer the information. In many cases, it's best to make only brief comments about your plans, especially if you are going to work for a competitor.
- *A statement of appreciation.* This too is optional. Thank your supervisor for his or her help, as long as you sincerely mean it. It's a nice way of saying that your decision to leave was prompted by other factors and you hope that you can maintain a good relationship.
- *Your resignation letter.* Hand in your resignation letter at this meeting. Comments made in the letter should jibe with what you say during the meeting.
- *Training a successor.* This isn't necessary, but it will help the boss to know if you will be around to train your successor. If

not, mention that you will leave a list of basic job duties and names of clients, contacts, or other essential people that your successor needs to know. You might even say you'll be available to answer questions by phone if this doesn't interfere with your new job.

• *Suggesting a replacement.* If your boss is receptive to a recommendation, go ahead and discuss who you have in mind. You may have a better idea of who can fill your shoes, offering your employer a prospect who wouldn't be considered otherwise.

During the conversation, there are several questions you may also ask:

• *Will you write a letter of recommendation?* Ask your boss to consider writing a letter of recommendation that you'll pick up before you leave. You're likely to get a better letter if it's written while you're still an employee. Many supervisors don't mind writing a letter, knowing it may cut back on the number of telephone calls from prospective employers who are checking on your job performance.

• *What additional work do you expect me to finish?* To avoid any misunderstandings or a last-minute rush, find out what you're expected to finish before you leave.

• *What will you tell prospective employers about my work?* If you're not certain that the boss will give you a good recommendation, find out during this meeting. Don't argue if you disagree with the boss's assessment of your work. Mention that you hope positive comments will also be made about your job performance, and list a few specific examples of your accomplishments. Finding out what the boss will say can help you decide whether to list this person as a reference or warn interviewers that unfavorable comments may be made that you can explain.

• *Are there any written or unwritten company policies about resigning that I should know about?* Among the basic matters to go over are arrangements for receiving your final paycheck, receiving compensation for unused vacation or sick days, retaining or selling company stock, and checking on retirement benefits. Find out how long health and life insurance coverage will continue and what to do if you want to retain the same policies.

• *Will I be considered for rehiring?* This information may come in handy should you ever consider working for the company again. Also, it's another indication of whether you will get a favorable job recommendation.

• *What is the procedure for turning in property that belongs to the company, including keys, a car, identification badge, uniforms, etc.?* Find out in advance how to return what belongs to your organization. It may be helpful to take care of everything before the last day when you're likely to be distracted by other matters.

Here is a sample conversation that gives you an idea of how smoothly this process can be handled:

EMPLOYEE: I've made a difficult decision, Jack—I've decided to resign. My last day will be two weeks from today on November 18. I've enjoyed working for you, but I've decided it's best for me to move on.

SUPERVISOR: I've known since your last performance review that you weren't happy with the way things have been going. What are you going to do?

EMPLOYEE: I accepted a job offer to work for Teltron.

SUPERVISOR: Well, I'm sorry things didn't work out here.

EMPLOYEE: I want you to know the Altmont project will be finished a week from Friday. That'll give you time to look it over before I leave.

SUPERVISOR: I appreciate that.

EMPLOYEE: I assume you'll want to fill my position as soon as possible.

SUPERVISOR: Absolutely.

EMPLOYEE: You might consider Linda. She did a terrific job covering for me while I was on vacation.

SUPERVISOR: Yeah, I'd forgotten about that.

EMPLOYEE: I have a favor to ask. Would you write a letter of recommendation for me? I know I won't need it now, but in the future it could come in handy. I'd like to pick it up the day I leave.

SUPERVISOR: Sure, I'll be happy to do that.

EMPLOYEE: Here's my letter of resignation for your files. Do you think I should talk to any other supervisor?

SUPERVISOR: Yes, I think my boss would like to know. Why don't you drop her a note or talk to her. You should notify the personnel department, too.

EMPLOYEE: OK, I'll do that. What about my final check? Will it be mailed to my house?

SUPERVISOR: Just ask personnel and they'll take care of it.

EMPLOYEE: Thanks for all your help, Jack. I'm going to miss you. I hope we can have lunch together before I leave.

Note the positive tone of this conversation. The comments are brief and to the point. The employer wants to know why this decision was made, but he's not offended by the statement that the employee needs to fulfill career goals. Think about how defensive he might have been if the employee had said, "I've really been bored the last six months and need to find more challenging work."

The conversation ends on a friendly note. If all goes well during your meeting, you'll be smiling when you conclude the session.

Of course, there may be a few unexpected curves thrown at you during the session. To prepare yourself, consider some common reactions:

The boss gets angry. Maybe your short-fused boss gets steamed that you have the audacity to leave. Remember that supervisors dislike employee turnover. They may worry about catching heat from their supervisors for losing people. And they know it's going to take time and extra effort on their part to replace you.

You may know your boss well enough to predict how he or she will react. If you anticipate a negative response, prepare yourself ahead of time. Steer the conversation away from sensitive subjects during your discussion. Accentuate the positive aspects of your tenure with the company.

Brace yourself for what may be said and try to keep your cool during the meeting. If the discussion becomes too heated, suggest that you postpone the talk until another time. However, if your boss loses it and asks you to clean out your desk and leave, do as told. You probably can't change his or her mind anyway. By maintaining your composure under these circumstances, your boss may even call you later to apologize.

The boss asks you to stay. Think twice before saying you'll even consider the prospect. There are too many people who have waffled and said they would stay, only to be let go later on the company's own timetable. If you're certain about your decision to leave, it's best to say "thanks but no thanks," even if you are "bribed" with a raise or promotion—unless money or a promotion is the sole issue. Mention that you have considered the pros and cons and have decided it's best for you to leave. Don't sound wishy-washy or your boss will assume you want to be talked out of your decision.

What to Do After the Official Word Is Out

As soon as you've taken care of the official resignation meeting, there are many unofficial matters that are equally important. Here are some of the most common:

Inform your colleagues. Talk to your colleagues and subordinates as soon as possible. If they have noticed things haven't been going well for you, they probably won't be shocked. You still owe them the courtesy of telling them you're about to become history. If they don't know why you're about to go, don't confide in them and tell the real reason if it's not something you've shared with the boss. Just keep it short and sweet and spend most of your time telling them how much you're going to miss them.

One management information system manager issued a memo, with management approval of course, to say he would stay until a replacement was found. He said that helped him let everyone in the company know exactly what he planned to do to avoid suspicion about his departure plans.

There may be a temptation to brag about leaving a bad situation for a much better job. Save all these comments for your family and friends. Your old colleagues won't feel better knowing you've escaped and they are left behind.

A study by Joel Brockner, a Columbia University Business School professor, found that employees' job satisfaction and commitment to their firms declined when they felt a co-worker left for a better job. Brockner explains that it's a situation where the people left behind feel they are stuck and may be envious of the person who is leaving for better opportunities.[1]

Inform customers, suppliers, and others outside the office. It goes without saying that you should be consistent in the statements made to this group, too. Maybe you don't think there's any harm in telling outsiders that your boss is a jerk, but that may just sound like sour grapes from someone who is about to leave.

Some people may expect their customers to follow them to their new job. Your customers may have even encouraged you to quit in the first place. But all too often, departing employees have been surprised at how few customers were willing to defect with them.

A Lasting Impression

The last impression you make at your company is as important as the first. By making a smooth transition, you will be in a much better frame of mind to get on with your life. Both your career and your personal reputation will benefit from a properly handled departure.

13

Making the Most of Your
Final Days at Work

In everything one must consider the end.
—Jean de La Fontaine

EVEN under the best of circumstances, the time between
the announcement of your resignation and your final day
at work can be emotionally charged. The key to a smooth
transition is to stay sensitive to the feelings and the needs
of those you will be leaving behind, while looking out for
yourself and preparing for the next phase in your work
life.

Making a graceful exit, like everything else, involves
planning. Here are a few suggestions about how to handle
your tenure as a lame duck.

Maintain good relationships with everyone.
Be prepared for different reactions to your departure.
Some people don't know how to say goodbye and may
avoid you as a result. Others may feel like they've been
"jilted" and will remain cool and aloof. Still others may
become uncharacteristically sentimental.

Treat everyone in a friendly, caring manner. Thank them

for their support and help. Let them know you hope to stay in touch.

Keep your cool.

Use good judgment in what you do and say during your final weeks on the job. Avoid confrontations with people you dislike. Be satisfied in knowing that you will soon be away from the problems and people who may have driven you to another job.

Don't start projects at your new job before leaving your old job.

Your new employer may try to persuade you to begin working before you leave your old job. But resist the temptation to make a good impression by saying yes. You won't do your best work serving two bosses. In the end, your new employer may question your abilities and your old boss will think you have shortchanged the company. You may even want to take a vacation between jobs in order to feel relaxed and refreshed.

Training Your Successor

Depending on the type of work you do and your position, you may be expected to train a successor. If that's the case, be sure to reserve enough time to thoroughly train your replacement, enabling that person to feel comfortable after you have left.

If you've encountered problems at the company, you may wonder how much you should say as fair warning to the new recruit. Should you take your successor aside as your trusted confidant and tell all? Or do you let this individual stumble into situations?

It's often best to take a neutral position. Let your replacement benefit from your experience and offer all helpful, pertinent information. But don't go on a tirade about the hassles you encountered or people to avoid, as you will end up wrongfully prejudicing this individual. Provide enough information so your successor won't stub his or her toe. But don't unload so much that the new employee will be tempted to run out the door—or straight to your supervisor with your criticisms.

Pass along as much information to your replacement as you would expect from someone training you. Gather information for a reference guide. Train your replacement so thoroughly that he or she will have few questions after you have left. However, you may want to be available by telephone to answer questions about important matters.

Do everything you can to help this person get off to a good start by putting things in order. This reflects your consideration for the company and for your replacement, which will be appreciated by everyone.

Here are some basic areas to cover with the person who takes over for you:

- Acquaint your successor with basic job duties, company policies, and expectations
- Go over a status report of all projects and include background information to offer a better understanding of what needs to be done
- Explain your filing system and where to find all resource materials
- Offer tips on the most efficient ways you found to complete your work
- Introduce your successor to others in the company; make a list of key personnel and their job titles, and draw up an organizational chart if it will be helpful
- Turn over a list of all job contacts, their addresses, and telephone numbers

- Take your replacement on a tour of the company to familiarize him or her with the location of key people and supplies
- Invite your replacement to special luncheons and get-togethers to help the individual get acquainted with others

The Exit Interview

Some companies will expect you to go through an exit interview. In some ways, it's almost like a debriefing. You're most likely to talk with your immediate supervisor, department head, or personnel director.

Companies may require exit interviews for different purposes. Some organizations use it to obtain information that will help pinpoint problem areas and problem people. If the departing employee was involved in sensitive financial matters, the interview may be part of an exit audit in which records are checked to avoid any questions about mishandled funds.

"We try to learn the reasons behind the decision to leave and how the organization could have dealt with what led up to the decision," said Dr. Dan Cohen, human resources director at the Trammell Crow Company, Dallas, Texas. He said the real estate development company, cited in *The 100 Best Companies to Work for in America,* considers what all departing employees say and checks to see if there is a pattern. The company looks for whatever helps improve organizational effectiveness. "We indicate that we want to help make the organization better," he said. This attitude sets the stage for interviewers to seek information and for departing employees to talk candidly.

An exit interview may take from five minutes to an hour, depending on what is discussed. Before the interview, you may want to ask your supervisor or the personnel department what is usually covered. In addition to the discussion, some companies also may ask you to fill out an exit interview form.

Some employees may have the option of refusing to participate in an exit interview. If you are leaving under less favorable circumstances and don't wish to discuss problems, ask if you can skip the interview. If you feel obligated to go through with it anyway, be careful about discussing sensitive information.

Typical questions asked during an exit interview are:

- Why are you leaving?
- Was the work too difficult?
- Did you have problems dealing with anyone?
- How would you improve the company?
- Were you properly trained?
- What did you like most about working here?
- What did you like least about the job?

In rare cases, a company official may even make an eleventh-hour offer to change conditions and persuade you to stay. Be careful about what you say, especially if the person conducting the interview is the one who prospective employers will call to ask about you. Your critical remarks may be taken the wrong way and result in an unfavorable recommendation you don't deserve.

A midlevel supervisor said that during exit interviews he always asked, "What don't you like about the company?" If a departing employee launched into a harsh critique, he resented what was said. He really didn't want to hear the negatives.

Be careful about what you say, especially if it falls into the unacceptable-reasons-for-leaving category. Keep in mind that what you say may be relayed to others. You can't be guaranteed confidentiality. It is best to make general comments in a constructive manner and address matters that can be changed or improved.

While this approach is prudent as a general rule, there are companies that go out of their way to be fair. At Kollmorgen Corporation, for example, employees are protected from recriminations, even when being critical, said James Ketcham, director of professional recruitment. "We won't give a bad reference to someone because they told the truth. We think honesty is the only way to treat people, and we expect them to treat us the same way."

The exit interview also gives you an opportunity to ask questions. You may want to find out if you will be considered for rehiring if you choose to return. Ask how the company will handle queries from other employers about your work performance.

Here is a brief excerpt from an exit interview with a personnel director:

PERSONNEL DIRECTOR: I'm sorry you're leaving us, Beth. I wish you well with your new job.

EMPLOYEE: Thanks, David.

PERSONNEL DIRECTOR: I'd like to find out a few things before you go. First of all, what prompted you to resign?

EMPLOYEE: I've been anxious to move from my administrative assistant's position into something different. Chances of doing that were limited. I was offered an opportunity to do that at my new job.

PERSONNEL DIRECTOR: Did anyone in particular block your path here?

EMPLOYEE: No, I can't single out anyone. I realized that a promotion was unlikely and I had gone as far as I could.

PERSONNEL DIRECTOR: What would you like to change about the company?

EMPLOYEE: I'd like to see the company offer more incentives to grow professionally. There were times when going to a seminar or having paid college tuition benefits would have motivated me to broaden my skills and stay with the company.

PERSONNEL DIRECTOR: What did you like best about your job?

EMPLOYEE: Overall, I had a good experience and learned a lot. I'm particularly glad I had a chance to work with my boss, Ms. Reynolds. She was fair and had a very supportive attitude.

The employee avoided harsh criticism of the company. She made general comments about the company rather than specific suggestions about her department. She focused on what was most appropriate to discuss with the personnel director. A discussion with her immediate supervisor might contain more comments about her particular work area.

Along with suggestions for improvements, the employee added comments about benefits of working for the company. As a result, the overall tone of her comments was positive.

Make a Clean Break

For some, breaking away from a company is hard to do. If your departure is the result of a better opportunity rather than an acrimonious split, you may find it difficult to let go of your job. You may be happy about a chance to further your career, but find it difficult to sever your ties with people you like. Some people even have trouble watching their successor take over for them.

The best break is a clean break. Try to avoid awkward moments when you might feel uncomfortable or sad in leaving. In some cases, even cleaning out your desk after working hours is advised. Be sure any unnecessary notes in files and "incriminating" information are packed up and carted out the door. Stay focused on the new opportunities that await you; move onward and upward.

14

If the Worst Happens

Get mad, but don't get even; get ahead.
—William J. Morin and
James C. Cabrera,
Parting Company

"I was sitting there in my boss's office getting nitpicked for the umpteenth time, when something snapped," Donna recalled. "Suddenly six months' worth of anger and frustration about working for this jerk started to boil over." Although she was tempted, Donna didn't want to quit at that moment, because despite her persistent efforts to find something else, nothing had turned up. Yet she couldn't sit there and take it another second. Without thinking, she simply stormed out of her boss's office, then left the building for the day. The next day she came back to work and her boss said, "What are you doing here? You're fired."

"I couldn't believe he'd fire me just like that," she said. But when she protested, her boss explained he was leery of keeping an employee after such an insubordinate act. He could no longer trust her, and it set a bad precedent for other employees as well. The fact was, things had been going badly, and he found the excuse he needed to fire her.

When the Boss Beats You to the Punch

What happens if you end up like Donna and the boss tells you to leave before you have a chance to quit? No matter whether you saw it coming or not, it is a gut-wrenching experience. The common reaction is: "How can someone do this to me? After all the hard work, overtime, and personal sacrifices?" In one swift blow, they take away your job, your identity, and a lot of your self-respect.

You can take some solace in the fact that you have plenty of company. One out of every four American workers will be fired from a job at some time during his or her career, according to a study by Robert Half International.[1] Of that group, 20 percent will not deserve to be dismissed. Some of the most successful people in business have gotten the ax. Yet the words "you're fired" are still two of the most dreaded words in the English language.

Once the boss decides to terminate you, it's unlikely that the decision can be reversed. Some people may seek to voluntarily resign or even go over their boss's head to plead for their job. But if tempers have flared and the boss has sent you packing, it's best to start making plans to clean out your desk.

In this kind of emotionally charged situation, it's wise to tell your boss that you will meet with him or her the next day to make final arrangements for your departure. You are in no condition to think clearly and discuss important matters, such as the amount of severance pay you should receive. It's best to get over the initial impact of being fired and then come back to take care of business matters.

Tell your boss that you would like to take the rest of the day off and schedule a time to meet again. Then leave rather than linger and wait for the word to filter around the office, or worse, stay and start bad-mouthing your boss.

It's usually best to go home and talk to your spouse, family members, or trusted friends. It helps to have someone around to confide in and discuss how you will deal with this abrupt change in your career.

Think twice before unloading your grief on your co-workers. Even if people agree your boss was difficult, keep your complaints to a minimum and discuss how you are going to find a much more satisfying job in the future. Begin networking immediately and enlist others to pass along information about job openings and contacts who can provide leads.

To Resign or Not to Resign

Some people are given the option to leave on their own terms and resign. The boss may have several motives for asking you to tender your resignation rather than firing you. Some of these may be purely altruistic. He or she may be helping you save face and avoid the humiliation of being canned. But the boss may also have self-interest at heart and know that persuading you to voluntarily resign can save the company a bundle of money in severance pay and other expenses.

When faced with this decision, weigh the consequences of being fired with the loss you may incur by agreeing to step down. One benefit of resigning is avoiding the stigma of being fired and facing more difficulty in getting hired elsewhere. It also may ensure better recommendations from your employer.

On the other hand, voluntarily resigning means that you will have to wait longer to receive unemployment benefits if you don't quickly land a job. You may not be eligible for severance pay or possible outplacement assistance if you leave on your own. Also, we know of many companies that give the person a chance to resign, but then leak the word that this person was asked to leave.

Don't let yourself get backed into a corner if you're given this option and aren't sure which way to go. Tell the boss you need more time to think about it before deciding what to do.

When Your Job Is Eliminated

It is an all-too-common scenario these days. A company undergoes a merger, cutback, or major change that results in eliminating hundreds, maybe even thousands of jobs. Employees nervously await the summons to the boss's office to find out if they're getting the next pink slip.

Increasingly large numbers of American workers are being cut loose in layoffs or offered early retirement. From the mid-1980s to 1990, nearly a million jobs were eliminated by major shifts in corporations.[2] Many of the jobs were white-collar positions, involving people who invested decades of their life at one company.

One consolation is that after enduring the turmoil of being laid off, many people find that their careers weren't ruined just because their company underwent a major reorganization. Some people have taken a cut in pay but gone to much more satisfying jobs. And others end up making more money and wondering why they waited so long before trying something different.

Often people see signs that their job is in jeopardy, but they decide to wait it out, hoping their position won't be cut. However, even if they survive, their troubles may not be over. They may still face changes that could include a new management team, a different corporate philosophy, and new policies. If you find yourself in this precarious situation and believe it's worth the gamble, then stay on. Just be careful that you look out for yourself.

This is especially true when a company has suffered major financial losses and may be in danger of going bankrupt. People are often torn between their loyalty to the struggling company and doing what is best for themselves. Leslie's story is typical of many we've heard: "A lot of us could see the end coming. First there were signs like our messenger service refusing to take any more deliveries because we were so behind on payments. Then we couldn't get anyone out to repair our copy machines unless we paid cash in advance. And finally there were rumors about not being able to make payroll. All the time, though, management kept telling us to hang in there, that we were going through a rough period but we'd pull out of it. I'd been with the company five years and it was hard for me to imagine it actually folding. Besides that, I wanted to believe management. Now I wished I'd gotten out earlier. Not only did the company fold, I lost two weeks' pay."

The Day After

When you and your boss have your final meeting, you may want to bring a list of questions to cover. If you aren't sure of what you're entitled to receive, check with the personnel department or with knowledgeable sources in your company to find out the maximum benefits. Here's what's generally available to terminated employees:

• Severance pay: Some organizations offer from two weeks' to a month's pay for every year you've been with the company. You may have the option of receiving severance money in a lump sum or in installment payments. If you're entitled to a fairly hefty amount of money, it may help your budget if you ask to receive several payments, similar to a paycheck, rather than get all the money at once and be subject to maximum tax penalties. Also, not everyone is in the right frame of mind after losing a job to wisely deal with a large sum of money.

• Vacation pay: You're entitled to get paid for the vacation time you have accrued. In some situations, you may even get extra pay for the compensatory time that you may not have taken.

• Pension, stock, and profit-sharing plan: Some plans have vesting that is determined by age and tenure at the company. Carefully look over your last financial statements to see what you have earned. If you have any questions, consult a good tax accountant to make sure you're receiving what you should and that you wisely transfer funds to an account that earns the most interest and will not be heavily taxed.

• Medical and life insurance coverage: Getting hit with high medical bills while you're out of work could be devastating, so make plans to continue major medical insurance. Once you leave a company with a group health insurance plan, you're protected by federal regulations that entitle you and your dependents to continue using the same policy. You will be charged the same premium rate as what your company is billed, which is often far less than what an individual policy with comparable coverage would cost. If you also want to get interim life insurance, check to see what term policies are available that have no cash value but simply provide protection.

• Maintaining an office and secretarial support: Some companies offer to help displaced employees by giving them temporary use of an office and the assistance of a secretary while they search for a job. This arrangement may be useful, if merely for appearance' sake, to have prospective employers telephone an office rather than a home. But before accepting an invitation to use this setup, ask yourself how you will feel showing up every day at the place where you used to work and facing people, even those who may have decided to terminate you.

Using Outplacement Services

More businesses are using outplacement programs to help terminated employees find another job and, equally important, deal with the psychological turmoil of being dismissed. And, companies which provide outplacement are less likely to be sued. Morale among remaining employees may be higher because they know their former co-worker is getting help in finding another job.

Most outplacement services provide one-on-one counseling, which covers coping with the emotional aspects of being fired or laid off, setting career goals, and launching a job search. The counselor may be at the company for a first meeting the day a person is terminated and then have meetings regularly throughout the entire job-search process. Follow-up sessions are held to discuss adjusting to the new job. This service isn't an employment agency—it doesn't provide job leads. But reputable outplacement companies help people put the pieces of their work life back together again.

Roughly one quarter of all outplacement clients start their own businesses or go into consulting, 29 percent go from a position in a large corporation to another large corporation, and 42 percent take jobs with smaller companies.[3] For people who are fifty-five or older, outplacement might make the difference between finding a new job or dropping out of the work force entirely. Some laid-off managers land jobs paying more than their former ones. They often find more job satisfaction, too, because the new position offers fresh challenges.

The Recovery Process

As terrible as the experience can be, getting fired or laid off serves as the push some people need to head them in the right direction. It has transformed unmotivated workers into productive employees, steered people into the right field, and helped entrepreneurs realize they needed to be on their own.

Still, there is no way to minimize the impact of getting fired. Sudden job loss is a big blow; it ranks among the major traumas in an individual's life. No one wants to terminate a working relationship under those circumstances. One feels a sense of failure, inadequacy, and personal loss. Many dwell too long on why they were fired, who was at fault, and on what they believe is the "utter injustice" of it all.

"I was trying desperately to get out of there anyway," a convenience store manager told me. "In fact, I'd just set up a job interview the day before my boss called me in and fired me. I didn't like the company, and I didn't like him, and my first reaction to getting fired was relief. I just said 'fine,' and I walked out of there like I couldn't have cared less. Then later on the fact that I'd just been unceremoniously dumped by the company bugged me. I didn't think it was fair. I began to feel that getting fired is kind of the ultimate rejection. I started to think I should have put up more of a fight. Raised a stink with upper management. Told my side of the story. Something."

What to Do about Employment Discrimination

Write or call the U.S. Equal Employment Opportunity Commission (EEOC) in Washington, DC, for a brochure on how to file a discrimination charge. If you have been discriminated against because of race, sex, religion, national origin, or age, you can file charges in person, by mail, or by telephone by contacting the nearest EEOC field office. The charges must be filed within 180 days of discriminatory acts, such as being turned down for a job, being denied a promotion or pay increase, or getting fired. The EEOC may file a lawsuit and/or an individual may file a private suit within 90 days of receiving a notice of right-to-sue from the EEOC.

I have counseled people who've spent months brooding over being fired. They wasted time that should have been spent in building up their confidence rather than tearing it down. The job hunt took much longer as a result.

When you are fired, there are many strong emotions to deal with, especially anger—anger toward yourself for waiting too long to make a move when you saw signs of trouble, and bitter feelings toward the person who let you go.

You can expect to experience a variety of emotions after losing a job. The cycle for most people who undergo this unhappy situation is:

Stage 1:   Relief in no longer having to cope with painful job problems

Stage 2:   Panic about loss of income and difficulty finding another job

Stage 3:   Anger at the employer for the firing

Stage 4:   Guilt about what contributed to job problems and concern about hardship on family

Stage 5:   Hopelessness about finding a better job

Stage 6:   Depression over prospects of a bleak future

Stage 7:   Acceptance of what happened

Stage 8:   Hope for bettering the situation

Stage 9:   Growth and knowledge from the experience

It is perfectly normal to go through all of these stages. In fact, if you don't feel the anger, guilt, frustration, and depression, it's unlikely that you will learn much from the experience. Some people get stuck in the hopeless and depressed state for too long before they reach the point of accepting the dismissal and getting on with their lives.

The important thing is to look back and learn from the situation. Shortly after the blowup, it's common to look back in anger and place the blame on the boss, thinking he or she was wrong and you were right. Then after a few days of reflection, you may think of ways the problems could have been avoided.

The quickest route toward recovery is to grow from the experience; to say that out of this adversity you have become more adept at managing your career and will know how to avoid this situation in the future. Apply that knowledge to finding a stable job and a group of people with whom you can work more effectively.

This experience can open up opportunities you never considered. Often people want to return to the same type of position, though it is not always possible and, in some situations, not advisable. Following an abrupt end to a job, you should take extra time for soul-searching, break away from familiar patterns, and seek a career track that will be more secure and rewarding.

Tomorrow's Outlook

As corporate America continues to restructure, firings and layoffs will become more common. As a result, there will be a different attitude about being let go. People will be more mentally prepared to deal with sudden job loss. Job interviewers will look more at an individual's specific accomplishments, rather than focus on résumés with a linear career path free of employment gaps.

Rapid changes in businesses will encourage employees to think and act more like independent contractors. They will not expect to find a paternalistic company to care and nurture them, and as a result, they will have less company loyalty than the organizational men and women of the past. But they will be highly productive and motivated to help the company while advancing their own careers. Greater awareness of career management will guide them in maximizing their potential.

Everyone in the work force can expect to experience ups

and downs in his or her career. Being able to deal with the upsets will help a person stay on track. Daniel Flynn, Lafarge Corporation's director of personnel services, summed up this thought by saying, "Everyone has had problems in life—some sooner than later, some more than others. The fact that one has had trauma in one's life is not as important as what one has done with it."

Postscript

WOULDN'T it be nice if there were some foolproof approach you could take every time you faced a major career transition? Then, voilà, your problems would be solved and the right choice would be crystal clear.

Unfortunately, it doesn't work that way. But we do believe that the process described in this book will make it easier to decide whether to quit or to stay in a job. By adopting these practices now, you will be prepared to steer your career through an even more volatile workplace in the twenty-first century.

Always remember to:

- Tackle job problems before they begin getting the best of you. Get to the source of the problem and find ways to resolve the difficulties.
- Make adjustments in your current job or seek a new position that allows you to use your greatest talents and skills so that you are always in the right job niche.
- Identify and select work options for yourself that are truly satisfying and meaningful.
- When considering two jobs, determine which one allows you to gain the most, lose the least.
- When quitting is the best option, resign in such a manner that you leave a good last impression.
- When staying and improving your job is the best option, adopt plans that allow you to continue growing professionally.

- If you are ever fired or laid off, learn from the experience and go on to a better job.

We wish you great success as you make your next move and later on when you are faced with other critical decisions.

Now we invite you to have the final word. The following questionnaire gives you an opportunity to share your decision with us. Your comments will be incorporated in subsequent editions of this book.

Send questionnaire to:

Before You Say "I Quit!"
c/o Collier Books
Macmillan Publishing Company
866 Third Avenue, 21st Floor
New York, NY 10022

Reader's Questionnaire

Check one: _____ Male _____ Female

City and state where you live: _____

Age: _____ Number of years at present job: _____

Occupation: _____

Job title: _____

How many jobs have you had during the past five years? _____

Why do you want to quit your job?

_____

_____

Have you decided to (check one) quit _____ or keep _____ your job?

If you leave, what type of work will you pursue?

_____

_____

Why did quitting appear to be the best choice?

_____

_____

_____

If you stay, what persuaded you to do so?

_____

_____

_____

If you stay, how will you improve your job?

_____

_____

_____

What part of the decision-making process was the most difficult?

_____

_____

_____

Notes

Introduction

1. From a survey of twenty-three thousand *Psychology Today* magazine readers, quoted by Salvatore V. Didato in *The Dallas Morning News,* Oct. 15, 1985.

2. From Bureau of Labor Statistics, quoted in "New Directions" by Leslie Barker, *The Dallas Morning News,* Dec. 19, 1988.

3. From *Calling It Quits* by Judith K. Sprankle, Bob Adams, Inc., 1985.

Chapter 1

1. From an interview with Dr. Richard Citrin.

2. From *The Dallas Morning News,* article by Christine Wicker, Feb. 10, 1987.

Chapter 2

1. From "The High Cost of Sexual Harassment" by Walter Kiechel, *Fortune,* Sept. 14, 1987.

2. From Paula I. Robbins, *Successful Midlife Career Change,* AMACOM, 1978.

3. From William E. Perry, *Orchestrating Your Career,* CBI Publishing Co., 1981.

Chapter 3

1. From Tom Jackson, "Living and Working in the 1990s," *Careers,* Sept. 1987.

2. From *The Dallas Morning News,* Nov. 22, 1988.

3. From Ronald L. Krannich, *Re-Careering in Turbulent Times,* Impact Publications, 1983.

Chapter 4

1. From Tom Jackson, "Living and Working in the 1990s," *Careers,* Sept. 1987.

Chapter 5

1. From "Business Fails to Fulfill Dreams of Baby Boomers" by Todd Vogel, *The Dallas Morning News,* Dec. 10, 1985.

Chapter 6

1. From "The Self-Made Man" by Teresa Carpenter, *Premiere,* Jan. 1989.

Chapter 8

1. From "How to Turn Your Company into Your Business School" by Jane Ciabattari, *Working Woman,* Dec. 1988.

Chapter 9

1. From Richard Bolles, *What Color Is Your Parachute?,* Ten Speed Press, 1983.

2. From Tom Camden and Nancy Bishop, *How to Get a Job in Dallas/Fort Worth,* Surrey Books, 1984.

3. Ibid.

4. Ibid.

5. Ibid.

Chapter 12

1. From "What About Workers Who Are Left Behind?," *The Wall Street Journal,* Jan. 15, 1988.

Chapter 14

1. From Joyce Lain Kennedy column, Sun Features, Inc.

2. From Beth Brophy, "You're Fired," *U.S. News & World Report,* March 23, 1987.

3. From interview with Ruth Glover, Plano, Texas, career consultant.

Bibliography

Anderson, Nancy. *Work With Passion.* New York: Carroll & Graf Publishers, 1984.

Arnold, John D. *Trading Up: A Career Guide.* Garden City, N.Y.: Anchor Press/Doubleday, 1984.

Baker, Nancy C. *Act II: The Mid-Career Job Change and How to Make It.* New York: Vanguard Press, 1980.

Banks, William C. "How to Negotiate a Job Transfer." *Money,* June 1984, 183–188.

Bardwick, Judith M. *The Plateauing Trap.* New York: American Management Association, 1986.

Blotnick, Srully. *The Corporate Steeplechase.* New York: Penguin Books, 1984.

———. "The Hidden Costs of Changing Jobs." *Working Woman,* June 1984, 91–95.

Bolles, Richard. *What Color Is Your Parachute?* Berkeley, Calif.: Ten Speed Press, 1983.

Brammer, Lawrence, and Frank E. Humberger. *Outplacement and Inplacement Counseling.* Englewood Cliffs, N.J.: Prentice-Hall, 1984.

Brooks, Andree. "Quitting a Job Gracefully." *New York Times,* Dec. 2, 1985.

Buskirk, Richard. *Your Career.* Boston: CBI Publishing Co., 1980.

Caple, John. *Careercycles.* Englewood Cliffs, N.J.: Prentice-Hall, 1983.

Carney, Tom. *Job Smarts: How to Play the Career Game.* New York: Facts on File, 1984.

Coulson, Robert. *The Termination Handbook.* New York: The Free Press, 1981.

Crystal, John, and Richard Bolles. *Where Do I Go from Here with My Life?* Berkeley, Calif.: Ten Speed Press, 1980.

Davidson, Jeffrey. "Controlling Staff Turnover." *Today's Office,* Aug. 1983, 23–24.

Deutsch, Arnold R. *How to Hold Your Job: Gaining Skills and Becoming Promotable in Difficult Times.* Englewood Cliffs, N.J.: Prentice-Hall, 1984.

Gordon, Thomas. *Leader Effectiveness Training.* New York: Wyden Books, 1977.

Haldane, Bernard. *Career Satisfaction and Success.* New York: AMACOM, 1981.

Helegesen, Sally. "When Should You Quit a Job—Or a Course?" *Glamour,* July 1984, 124.

Holland, John. *You and Your Career.* Odessa, Fla.: Psychological Assessment Resources, 1977.

———. *Making Vocational Choices: A Theory of Vocational Personalities and Work Environments.* Englewood Cliffs, N.J.: Prentice-Hall, 1985.

Howell, Barbara. *Don't Bother to Come in on Monday.* New York: St. Martin's Press, 1973.

Irish, Richard K. *Go Hire Yourself an Employer.* New York: Anchor Books, 1978.

Jaffe, Dennis T., and Cynthia D. Scott. *Take This Job and Love It.* New York: Simon & Schuster, 1988.

Johnson, Greg, and Thomas M. Rohan. "Why Executives Jump Ship." *Industry Week,* April 1982, 62–64, 66, 70.

Krannich, Ronald L. *Re-Careering in Turbulent Times: Skills and Strategies for Success in Today's Job Market.* Manassas, Va.: Impact Publications, 1983.

Kriegel, Robert, and Marilyn Harris Kriegel. *The C Zone.* New York: Anchor Press, 1984.

Levering, Robert, Milton Moskowitz, and Michael Katz. *The 100 Best Companies to Work for in America.* Reading, Mass.: Addison-Wesley, 1984.

Lewis, Adele, and Bill Lewis. *How to Choose, Change, Advance Your Career.* New York: Barron's Educational Series, 1983.

Michelozzi, Betty Neville. *Coming Alive from Nine to Five.* Palo Alto, Calif.: Mayfield Publishing Co., 1984.

Morin, William J., and James C. Cabrera. *Parting Company.* New York: Harcourt Brace Jovanovich, 1984.

Noer, David. *Jobkeeping: A Hireling's Survival Manual.* Radnor, Pa.: Chilton Book Company, 1976.

Perlov, Dadie. "How to Change Partners and Dance." *Association Management,* November 1982, 92–93.

Perry, William E. *Orchestrating Your Career.* Boston: CBI Publishing Co., 1981.

Plumez, Jacqueline Horner. *Divorcing a Corporation.* New York: Villard Books, 1985.

Potter, Beverly A. *Maverick Career Strategies: The Way of the Ronin.* New York: American Management Association, 1984.

Reif, Robin. "Breaking Up (With Your Job) Is Hard to Do." *Mademoiselle,* March 1984, 152.

Robbins, Paula. *Successful Midlife Career Change.* New York: AMACOM, 1978.

Sheehy, Gail. *Passages.* New York: Bantam Books, 1976.

Sherwood, Andrew. "How to Resign Effectively." *Supervisory Management,* June 1984, 22–24.

Sprankle, Judith K. *Calling It Quits.* Boston: Bob Adams, 1985.

Stewart, Nathaniel. *Help Your Boss & Help Yourself.* New York: AMACOM, n.d.

Talley, Madelon. *Career Hang Gliding: A Personal Guide to Managing Your Career.* New York: E. P. Dutton, 1986.

Townsend, Robert. *Up the Organization.* New York: Alfred A. Knopf, 1970.

Uris, Auren. *Thank God It's Monday.* New York: Thomas Y. Crowell, 1974.

Vogel, Todd. "Business Fails to Fulfill Dreams of Baby Boomers." *Dallas Morning News,* December 10, 1985.

Wareham, John. *Secrets of a Corporate Headhunter.* New York: Atheneum, 1980.

Weiss, Donald H. *How to Negotiate a Raise or Promotion.* New York: AMACOM, 1986.

Wheeler, D. D., and Janis Wheeler. *A Practical Guide for Making Decisions.* New York: The Free Press, 1980.

Zey, Michael. *The Right Move.* New York: Franklin Watts, 1987.